You Got
Magic

You Got Magic

NEEL MADHAV

WITH VINITA MADHAV

PENGUIN BOOKS

PENGUIN BOOKS

USA | Canada | UK | Ireland | Australia
New Zealand | India | South Africa | China

Penguin Books is part of the Penguin Random House group of companies
whose addresses can be found at global.penguinrandomhouse.com

Published by Penguin Random House India Pvt. Ltd
7th Floor, Infinity Tower C, DLF Cyber City,
Gurgaon 122 002, Haryana, India

First published in Penguin Books by Penguin Random House India 2016

10 9 8 7 6 5 4 3 2 1

ISBN 9780143334521

Book design by Neelima P Aryan
Typeset in Avenir by R. Ajith Kumar, New Delhi
Printed at Thomson Press India Ltd, New Delhi

www.penguinbooksindia.com

Contents

Introduction
THE BIG REVEAL

So, I've written a book. Well, *sort of*. A person who wanted to get away from numbers and digits and words and sentences has written a book! And if you think I'm absolutely stoked about it—don't. Because I'm really not. I had no clue about what to write or how to start. But I think you should continue reading anyway, because rarely will you get to read a book that starts with the author confessing how absolutely clueless they are about what comes next.

It's almost like you're sitting down to take an exam. You walk into this room, bubbling with nervousness, everyone else walking in with you in total silence. You can hear the indistinct murmurs—someone revising, someone ardently praying. Everyone then sits down on their respective chairs. You start looking around, maybe even exchange a brief smile with those sitting next to you. And five minutes into the whole scene, while you wait for the question paper, you have already figured everything out. When I say everything, I mean everything that makes up your process and your approach. And while all this happens, there is only one thing that's going on in your head—you're hoping that the paper is easy. Then the question paper starts getting distributed and the whole room tenses up, everyone is focused. It's almost like a race—who writes longer answers, who uses more answer sheets, who finishes the fastest. Then you finally read the questions and start making mental notes about how you're going to start,

what you're going to write, how you're going to conclude. That's exactly what I'm doing right now. And you are diving into my brain to see how it works.

As you read on, you will discover the mental notes that I make to help the magic come alive in my mind and onstage. You see, when I am on that stage, I have to reveal enough of my art to make you curious but also hide enough of it to keep that curious mind of yours hooked. But here I'm bringing to you all of the techniques that are always hidden from view. You see the irony? I'm revealing something that should not be revealed! And for you to learn this art, you should bring not only your passion, but also great discipline and practice. Magic will bring you the unexpected but also hone your personality and communication skills.

But before you start reading about the simplicity and sublimity of magic, do as I ask you to—

Think of the first time you remember seeing magic. I don't want you to think about what you saw, but I want you to remember how the magic made you feel.

How did it make you feel?

And why did it make you feel like that?

Cracking the Codes

KNOW YOUR DIFFICULTY LEVEL

QUEEN	KING	ACE	ACE PLUS

EASY	MEDIUM	HIGH	VERY HIGH

KNOW YOUR VIEW

SPECTATOR'S VIEW IN A **BLUE FRAME**

CONCEALED VIEW IN AN **ORANGE FRAME**

Finding Magical Roots in the Lower Himalayas

What is my kind of magic? My kind of magic is young, contextual and engaging.

But where did my journey with magic start?

Was I a child producing pigeons out of an empty box at the age of ten, and impressing girls with card tricks at parties as a lanky teenager? Or was I a quiet, introverted young lad who always wondered about what lay beyond the real world—a world of illusion, perhaps?

The answer is—none of the above!

Magic is a part of my life and persona. I am intrigued by magic and have been mesmerized by magicians, some of whom I have had the good fortune to meet from around the world, spending hours on end with them—sometimes even twenty at a stretch—practising and mastering the art.

I believe it's my turn now to pass on the incredible excitement and mystery of magic to those keen to partake in it.

1

As a child, I'd often wondered what it would be like to live in a valley enveloped by majestic mountains on all sides. Where the sun would shine from behind the peaks, where there would be the true green of leaves and trees.

At twelve, I found my childhood fantasy coming true as I entered the gates of the prestigious Doon School in Dehradun. To fulfil my dream, I had to study hard and pass a tough entrance test as well as an interview, but I'd finally made it! The overwhelming facade of the red-ochre building, framed by watchful deodars, pines and conifers, represented a faraway world—completely distinct from the urban jungles of Mumbai and Delhi, which I was used to. A world not just about academics, but also about sports, music, hobbies and camaraderie—all in one place. As I stepped inside the portals of the Doon School, I could sense, somehow—even at that young age—that this association would be momentous for me. And, indeed, it was.

Soon enough, I found myself in my new home within this world—Hyderabad House, one of the oldest houses in the Doon School. The big windows of the study rooms overlooked the sprawling grounds. As I walked through the house, I realized that it was a strange labyrinth of corridors, dormitories, seniors' rooms, and study rooms called *Toye* rooms. I found myself ensconced in a rather large dormitory which I shared with eight other boys who were the same age as me. I had a simple bed along with a side table to myself. Very spartan, as there were no air conditioners or air coolers. Just old-fashioned fans, whirring noisily.

It took me no time to blend in with the academic and sporting traditions of Doon, since I was surrounded by kids just like myself—young boarders who had left home to grow up to be confident men. We were trained and tutored to do everything ourselves—make our beds, stack our clothes neatly, polish our shoes till they shone, keep our study materials in an organized manner in the Toye. Unlike its name, the Toye room—that housed our study desks and where we did our homework—had no toys. 'Toye time' was a serious two-hour study session after dinner. Now *that* took some getting used to!

Life at the Doon School was by no means luxurious. We were not allowed mobile phones, pocket money or even what every teenager took for granted—a pair of jeans. A laptop was only allowed during study hours, not after that. Therefore, there was no browsing of various websites that otherwise comes naturally to any teen. But, as we grew older, we found our way around that as well. A telephone call using a 'phone chit' once a week was our only connection with the outside world. And a weekly trip to the city centre—in our formal uniforms—with just Rs 350 to spend very judiciously, was our experience of a day out. Our money was mostly spent on food or movies—our thoughts were far removed from the lure of branded clothing and expensive restaurants. Our outings, as mentioned, were mostly about food, food and more food! Come to think of it, boarders are probably the hungriest boys alive. The town of Dehradun is very small and only two or three eateries were our regular haunts. We'd either go to a popular fast-food joint, called Nirulas, for burgers, the Hotel President for lunch, or a pizza place for a big meal! And wherever we'd go, we went as one big noisy group of boys! As we grew older, though, it would become a big noisy group of Doon School boys and Welham girls. Perhaps this overall lack of indulgence at Doon was one of the reasons why so many of us could go on to achieve so much in life.

Along with the school ethos, our uniforms are rather iconic too. We had one set for the school hours, a multicoloured set for the sports hours, kurta-pyjamas to be worn at dinner, and grey formalwear for our trips into town. Our formalwear had to be accompanied by polished black shoes, making us stand apart from the rest of Dehradun—rivalled only by our neighbours at the prestigious Indian Military Academy. There goes a Dosco—all would say to us!

Gradually, I made some good friends and we were always there for each other, despite the ghosts of 'sneaks'—boys who were in the habit of telling tales about the others to the housemaster or the house captain—lurking around the corridors. Once school hours ended, we would be left with enough time to frolic around, play games or even pursue our favourite pastimes. In time, the lively school environment forged many friendships among us boys, while some of us also learnt to be our own companions and best friends. I engaged myself with football, cricket and gymnastics, going on to become the school captain of the gymnastics team. The silent rigour of gymnastics trained my body and my mind to focus without distraction.

While sports assumed centre stage in my life, I also took to music—

particularly to the sitar, under the able guidance of my guru, whom we called GSS. He was also Housemaster of Hyderabad House and quite a personality. Tall and rather well built, his moustache twitched funnily sometimes, which often made my face break into a silent smile. My teacher was passionate about music as well as cricket; he was also the master in charge of cricket. It was due to GSS that, in the eighth grade, I was introduced to the sitar—without even knowing *what* the sitar was. And what a funny story there is behind it!

One fine morning, all the kids in the eighth grade who had opted for music were seated in the music room, when GSS started asking everyone what instrument we wanted to learn. When it was my turn, he asked me about my preference in a rather loud voice and, confused and scared, I froze.

The instrument that I had imagined in my head was the sarangi. I could recognize the sound it made, even knew what it looked like—but I didn't know what it was called. What a dilemma! But the closest, coolest, name that came to mind at that moment was the sitar. And that's how I started learning the sitar—all the time thinking it was the sarangi!

Learning to play the sitar was no easy task. At times, it even got really boring. I had to sit in a room and practise for hours and hours until I got the technique right. Sometimes I had to refine the same tedious technique over and over again without being able to make head or tail of the reason behind doing it. Imagine watching a movie about learning kung fu in which the master makes the student do something absolutely irrelevant and mindless, only to later realize the genius behind the torture! As a student, once you realize how brilliant the move is, you pat yourself on the back for not giving up and keeping faith in your teacher. *That* is when you feel motivated. You realize that you can do something that you couldn't before. This gives you confidence, driving you to work even harder.

After a point, when I'd got acquainted with the strings, I started making my own music. I started innovating! GSS instilled in us the painstaking rigour behind the complicated finger movements, and we learnt to concoct a soulful melody with the notes. That is how my love affair with music began. The school orchestra, of which I was a part, was an exercise in sheer creativity and an extension of GSS's musical genius which had rubbed off on us all. For the Founder's Day celebrations, the show by the orchestra was one of the main events, and we had to practise long hours to perfect our performance. Practising anything relentlessly—albeit sports or music—became the students' mantra for success in every field.

I'd spend hours in the music school and strangely enough, it was perhaps, in some way, music that led me to magic.

The place where we would practise our lessons had a lot of rubber bands lying around among the stationery, with which we would tie up our music sheets. Whenever someone would muck up during a symphony, and would need to get their notes right, I would put down my sitar and start playing around with the rubber bands. Eventually it would be this playful engagement that would help me segue into the world of magic.

School was really disciplined, but we didn't mind because we'd find a way around all the rules! I guess that's how we really learnt the things that are worth learning. Everyone asks me why I liked boarding school so much and, after much pondering, I realized that I enjoyed it because most of my education was outside the classroom. I guess that's how I preferred to learn and still do.

The house common room was where we occasionally had our brief spells of watching television. One day, when I was in the tenth standard, I had watched this magician on TV performing magic tricks with—what else but—rubber bands! 'Two solids cannot pass through each other . . .?' said the magician, but he had done almost the exact opposite—the bands seemed to go *through* one another. In fact, he had one band locked inside the loop of the other as if the solid rubber of one had magically passed through the rubber of the other band. Thus they'd merged into one—but I just couldn't figure out how!

The act intrigued me greatly and got me thinking. And after days and days of agonizing thought, and the perseverance that was instilled in me, I deconstructed the trick. I realized that it required quick finger movements, a thorough understanding of the pattern of movements that one had to follow and, of course, meticulous practice to get the motion right. It became clear to me that it's actually the swiftness of the pattern that creates the illusion of one solid passing *through* another. And this trick is most commonly known as the Law-defying Rubber Bands!

Law-defying Rubber Bands

Linking two rubber bands

MATERIAL REQUIRED:
Two size 19 rubber bands of different colours.

PREPARATION: **Place the spectator directly in front of you. The position of the thumb should be exactly at the same level as the spectator's line of vision.**

THE TRICK DECODED

1. Ask the spectator to inspect the rubber bands.

2. Loop one rubber band on both your index fingers, and one on both your little fingers. Move your hands apart, stretching the bands.

3. You will have four lengths, two of each rubber band. Take the second and third strings, and twist them, intertwining both. This will leave you with two knots on either side. The knots have to be held in place by the middle and ring finger of each hand.

4. However, the fingers conceal the knot and the rubber bands appear just as they were since the spectator should only see the back of your hands.

5. Now ask the spectator to pinch the second and the third strings, rubbing the node repeatedly. To heighten the suspense of the trick, tell them that this will generate heat, melting the rubber and fusing the bands together.

6. While they are doing this, release the rubber band from the middle and ring fingers of your right hand. This will make the knot shift to the middle, linking the rubber bands together!

⑦ Now you can also go on to ask the spectator to rub the knot again. While they do so, release the knot from your left hand, unlinking the rubber bands!

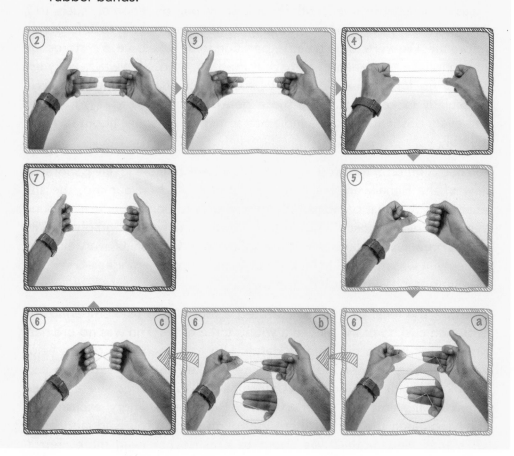

At Doon, our end-of-term examinations would be followed by biannual trekking trips called mid-terms—once in the month of April, and then again in September. These five-day-long trips were always eventful. The class would be divided into groups, and seven or eight of us young lads would start planning our excursion to the mountains while still sitting for our exams! We would be given a paltry amount of money with which we had to sensibly account for everything—taxis, local buses, a tour guide, food and even an occasional bath. We would mostly be roughing it, so to speak, and would be accompanied by one of the younger school teachers to keep an eye on us. Often, our teachers would end up becoming our friend. On one particular trip, our history teacher—who was also a

very talented sportsman—joined us. And, till date, he has remained my favourite teacher.

I was halfway into the tenth standard when, on another such trip, an extraordinary event in an unremarkable garb was waiting to unfold itself before me. We were to go on an expedition to Renuka Lake, a picturesque location close to Nahan in Himachal Pradesh. And, as always, we were gearing up for the exciting, exotic experience that lay ahead of us. I particularly looked forward to these getaways since I'd always believed that every destination across India has something magical about it. And I still do!

Perched high on a forested ridge, Renuka Lake offers a lovely panoramic view of the Himalayan peaks in the distance. And on our trip, the site resembled a virtual paradise! Summer was in full bloom and all around were birds of the most exotic kind, which we eagerly photographed. Wild berries grew in abundance and nature allowed us to relish its every element in plenty. It was magical! In fact, we still cherish our memories—by way of the photographs—of our time there.

One day, the local tour guide narrated a folk tale to us, comparing the twittering cuckoo of the hills to a young girl. This cuckoo was no ordinary bird—it was a little girl named Haruli. She had been sent to the fields to pick berries for her mother. As she plucked the berries in the sun, she played with her rag doll. Unfortunately, the berries she collected shrank by the time she returned home! Her mother, angry, accused her of having eaten the best of them. Although Haruli professed innocence, her disbelieving mother was about to chastise her even more. Terror-stricken, Haruli ran away, shrinking into the form of a bird! And she flew away across the sky. Later, as evening fell, the moist breeze wafted by and the wilted berries swelled in their basket to their original size. The young girl's bereft mother, seeing that she had erred, was overcome with remorse. She, too, was transformed into a bird, and followed her lost daughter in the skies. One bird called penitently that the berries were still ripe, and the other endlessly pleaded that she hadn't been greedy.

This, too, was a story about the unbelievable, much like the rubber bands in my hands! No one could believe that I had actually merged two into one, or stretched and passed them through each other.

Listening to the tale, I gulped down a handful of berries myself to try the move with the rubber bands again. And again, the two bands merged into one. After a lot of practice, I was executing my first magic trick!

Excited, I tried another variation of the rubber band trick.

Freaky Jumping Band

A rubber band shifts from the magician's hand to the spectator's hand

MATERIAL REQUIRED:
Four identical size 19 rubber bands.

PREPARATION: Wear three–four rubber bands around your wrist. The trick will be performed with only one of them.

THE TRICK DECODED

1. Wear a rubber band around your right wrist and stretch it across your palm with the fingers of your left hand.

2. Give the band a twist and lock it between the thumb and index finger of your right hand.

3. Putting one loop of the rubber band right around the top of your thumb, stretch it further to wrap it around the fingers.

4. Now you have two loops of the same rubber band—one around your wrist and the other around your four fingers.

5. Ask the spectator to put their hand forward, placing their palm on

top of the back of your hand. Place your left hand above your and the spectator's hands.

⑥ Snap the fingers of your left hand to time the effect and simultaneously release the loop around your right thumb. The rubber band will jump to the spectator's hand—around their fingers!

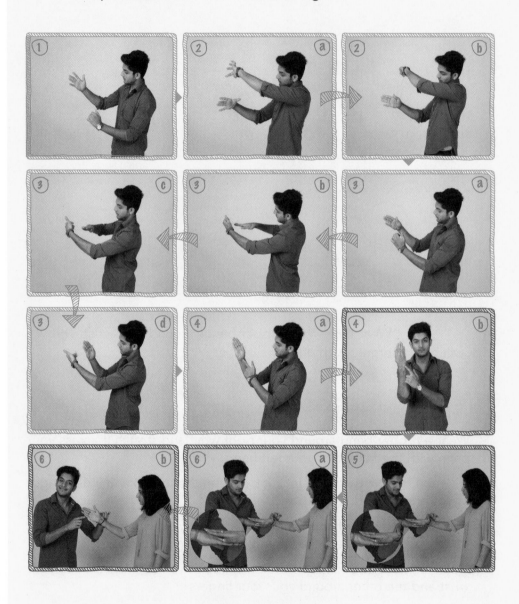

The legend of the Vanishing Hitch-hiker is very well known. And the vanishing rubber band is a version of the same legend, don't you think? In the American urban legend of the hitch-hiker, an ordinary-looking man or woman stops vehicles for a lift in the middle of a deserted motorway. Once they get in the car, they engage the driver in conversation. The magical—in this case, spooky—part occurs when, right before being dropped at their destination, the hitch-hiker vanishes from the vehicle—in the dark of the night or in the thick fog.

Rubber bands are like this hitch-hiker. They are a modern-day legend that can bend, twist, change form and vanish at the blink of an eye! Rubber bands can be easily found in people's pockets or anywhere within reach.

So if you can manipulate rubber bands in any fashion—and that's so much fun—imagine what would happen when you use the same rubber bands to manipulate people's minds!

I tried this trick with all my closest friends at Doon for the first time. I used to wear a lot of coloured rubber bands under my wristband and even under friendship bands. So the mystery of the jumping rubber band would be played out in the dormitory often. And what a feeling it was to see the look of sheer awe in the eyes of my young housemates—worth a million dollars! And this was another way by which I forged friendships with my housemates—especially my juniors! While I performed for my friends, each one would try to catch me out, and, so, I had to carry out my hand movements as smoothly as possible! On most occasions, I succeeded and got lots of thumps on the back, but there were also instances when my tricks failed. At times like those, I used to feel crestfallen—but my mates still encouraged me. And that motivated me to practise even more. I guess it's this sort of support that makes the camaraderie in a boarding school truly unparalleled.

Sports at the Doon School is taken very seriously and the inter-house competitions are fought fiercely by each of the houses. For us, there was no question of taking it easy. An intense feeling of competitiveness among the students was backed by a willingness to practise hard and strategize cleverly. The opposition's strengths were reviewed before every match, each rival player was assessed and then the game plan was made. All of this was primarily done by the boys themselves.

An abiding memory of our fellowship is an incident that occurred when I was still a junior. The end of term was upon us—our exams were over, the results were out—and it was time to go home, having spent four months at school. We were all set to catch the buses to Delhi in the morning. The night before, enthusiasm was at its peak and a sense of anticipation gripped us all. Psyched at the prospect of going home soon, the seventeen of us in the junior dormitory decided to play French cricket indoors! Amidst much shouting and cheering, the game got under way. But, unfortunately, one of the boys hit a crazy shot at one of the large windowpanes. And the glass came crashing down! At once we stopped playing, looking at each other furtively. There was pin-drop silence as we all stared mutely at the shattered glass.

One of the junior boys from another dormitory, in order to avoid getting into any trouble himself, went off sneakily to report the matter to the housemaster and the deputy headmaster. And soon enough, both gentlemen arrived at the scene of the crime and started interrogating us. The big question was, 'WHODUNNIT?' Seventeen poker-faced boys—all in the age group of fourteen to fifteen—were the suspects. But the deputy headmaster and housemaster were faced with young boys who just would not talk. Questioning gave way to threats and, finally, to an ultimatum.

'Unless someone owns up to the crime or someone else brings us the name of the culprit, all seventeen boys will be barred from going home in the morning!'

What an incredibly high price to pay for a bit of enthusiasm! The scene was one to behold. Two stern school authorities, several teachers, a few senior boys—including the house captain—and seventeen hapless fourteen-year-olds!

And without a word being exchanged, the 'bro code' took over—the 'don't-ever-squeal-on-your-housemate' principle came into effect. Nervousness turned to team spirit and no one budged. We were all in it together and we would collectively suffer for it if required. The ties that formed during that ordeal would go on to bind us together for the rest of our lives. Many of us reunite from time to time even today, the matter of geography and time is only incidental.

Boarding school is an experience like no other. Those who've never attended one might think it's just like the school in the Harry Potter series. This wasn't Hogwarts and there were no mean kids around who could cast mean spells. But these friendships were also real, solid and definitely worth cherishing. This was because we were all thrown into situations that made us value each other more than anything else around us. Think about it—here was a residential school, where all kinds of kids from different backgrounds come together to study and grow up. We shared experiences that we can return to over and over again for the rest of our lives.

Just like the following trick, which is still discussed by all my form-mates whenever we meet as I had rehearsed it with them so many times!

Coins are easy to find . . . but what do you do when someone wants an extra coin? Remember, coin tricks require a lot of initial practice!

The Mystery of the Extra Coin

Plucking a coin out of thin air

MATERIAL REQUIRED:
Any coin.

PREPARATION: **Place the spectator directly in front of you. The position of the thumb should be exactly at the same level as the spectator's line of vision.**

1. Hold the coin with your index finger and middle finger on one side and the thumb on the other.

2. Flip the coin by 90 degrees so that it can be gripped by your middle and index fingers.

3. Transfer the coin to the groove between your index finger and thumb. In this position, the coin is invisible to the spectator.

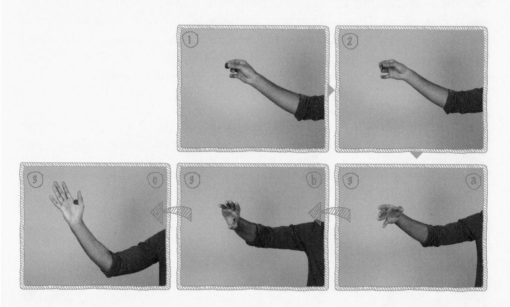

THE TRICK DECODED

1. In a quick motion, flip the coin up and hold it with your middle finger, index finger and thumb.

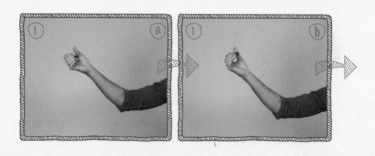

14

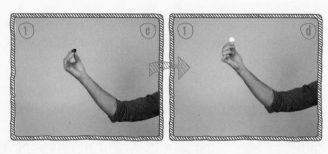

THE EXECUTION

Neel's Tip: As this illusion is based on sleight of hand, the move must be polished till it's perfect!

I had one particular experience at Doon that was far more eventful than anything else in my entire school life, and is worth sharing with everyone.

Once we were in our senior years—from the tenth standard onwards—the schoolmasters used to encourage us to undertake more ambitious trekking expeditions during our mid-terms. The planning and execution—ingrained in us by the strategizing skills and team-building exercises we'd learnt on the sports field—were meticulously done by the boys. During one of my senior years, we were debating hard about which destination we should go to—the choice was between Roopkund Lake and the Yamunotri Glacier.

Roopkund is at a height of 8000 feet, and used to fall on the erstwhile trading route between India and Tibet. Legend has it that Roopkund is the abode of Shiva and Parvati. It is said that the Goddess had felt thirsty and Lord Shiva, happily obliging, created a kund or a lake full of water. There is an even stranger, mysterious aura surrounding Roopkund, as there are over 200 skeletons strewn around it, which can be seen when the ice melts. In 1942, a lone forest ranger had come upon this vast grave, sparking intense speculation. Who were they? Were they a Tibetan tribe who had been buried under the snow or an army from the 15th century? These and several others are the stories that characterize Roopkund. Many other more plausible theories also add to the enigma of Roopkund. And all of these were narrated to us by our master-in-charge.

Yamunotri, on the other hand, is the source of the holy Yamuna River and is at an altitude of 11,000 feet, high up in the Garhwal Himalayas. A few kilometres away is the Champasar Glacier. Popular lore claims that Yamuna is the daughter of Surya, the Sun god, and the river emanates from a mountain next to it, called the Kalind Parvat—Kalind being another name for Surya. The beauty of the glacier and its surroundings is spellbinding.

The master in charge of the trip, who was advising us about the possible destinations, talked highly of both places. And so, we split into two teams of six boys each. While one went to Roopkund to hunt for ghosts, my team went to Yamunotri to find divine inspiration.

We carried all our rations, clothing and sleeping bags in our rucksacks, carefully planning the destinations we had to reach at the end of each day. The climb up from Uttarkashi was mesmerizing, gentle in some places and very steep in others. A stone path meandered through hamlets, fields, rivulets and waterfalls. This trek took us across mountains topped with clouds, where the sunrays streamed filtered through conifers; there was a chill in the air. We wondered what lay ahead of us. The following day, a light drizzle created a rather slushy path, and soaked our clothes and numbed our bodies. Yet we kept marching ahead.

That rainy night, our guide helped us find an abandoned hut to sleep in, some dry twigs to light a fire with and cups of hot chai to warm us. Sleep was all that we needed and none of us minded the fact that we were in a rather smelly hut! We zipped ourselves up in our sleeping bags, with no pillows and no duvets, dozing off as soon as our heads hit the snug bags. We were woken up the next morning by the chirping of the birds. The dawn arrived with faint rays of the sun peeping through the clouds. Not too far away, the snow-clad mountains were glistening, resplendent in the morning sun.

That afternoon, two of us—myself and my friend—got lost, and it was only towards the end of the day that both of us were reunited with our friends! It was a nervous time as we kept trying to find the way to our destination in the mountains. As we plodded along the narrow stone path, we didn't meet anybody for hours together, which added to our anxiety. But this kind of solitude also forces you to find a way, and find a way we both did!

It was during this arduous search for our group, that I found some coins in my pocket. Soon, in order to overcome the tension, I started playing around with the coins—making them magically appear and disappear. I could not help but smile at the irony of it all—here I was lost in the mountains, and I was making coins appear and disappear! I wished that I could do the same with myself—or the path. Finally, after three hours, my friend and I met two village boys who gave us some directions. It still took us a couple of hours more to get back on the correct mountain trail. That evening, when we found our friends, who had been equally anxious, I lightened the mood by demonstrating my new-found dexterity with coins. We dubbed it the 'Treasure in the Air'.

Everyone thought that the two of us would arrive looking anxious, but we didn't let it show! On our way down from the glacier, as we stopped at a dhaba to drink some chai, I resumed humouring everyone. I told them the story of the coin that would magically return to its owner, the *inkluz*, and the spoon that would twist on its own, spookily returning to its original shape! Not only did I regale my co-trekkers with these tales, I also astonished them with my latest coin trick!

Treasure in the Air

Pulling dozens of coins from nowhere and even letting a spectator produce one

MATERIAL REQUIRED:
An opaque mug or glass, and a handful of coins of the same denomination.

PREPARATION: Just before the performance, cup the coins in the fingers of your left hand, and then pin them against the inside of the glass. This conceals the coins from the spectator. Now, with your left thumb, hold the glass from the outside, at the rim. Then, using the Classic Palm Technique, palm a coin in your right hand. Your gimmick is ready!

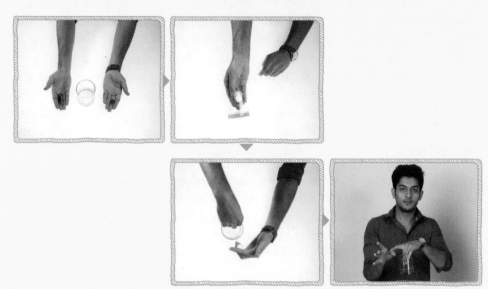

THE TRICK DECODED

① Begin the trick by pushing the palmed coin into view with your right thumb. This looks like producing a coin from thin air!

② Display the empty glass to the spectator—the coins being concealed by your fingers.

③ Now perform the illusion of dropping the coin you just produced in the 'empty' glass. For this, you'll have to insert your fingers inside the glass to make it look like you're depositing the produced coin. But what you actually have to do is transfer the coin back into the classic palmed position in your right hand while simultaneously lifting the fingers of your left hand just enough so that one coin visibly falls to the bottom of the glass.

④ Repeat the same sequence of actions over and over again, and keep producing coins from wherever you deem possible—the spectator's ears, nose, even elbows! The trick, thus, is actually producing the same coin over and over again!

⑤ For the finale, when you have just one remaining coin kept hidden by the fingers of your left hand, tell the spectator to imagine producing a coin from thin air and to toss the imaginary coin towards the mug.

⑥ Watch and trace the invisible path of the imaginary coin and as it reaches the mug, release the last coin in your left hand at the perfect time and leave the spectator amazed!

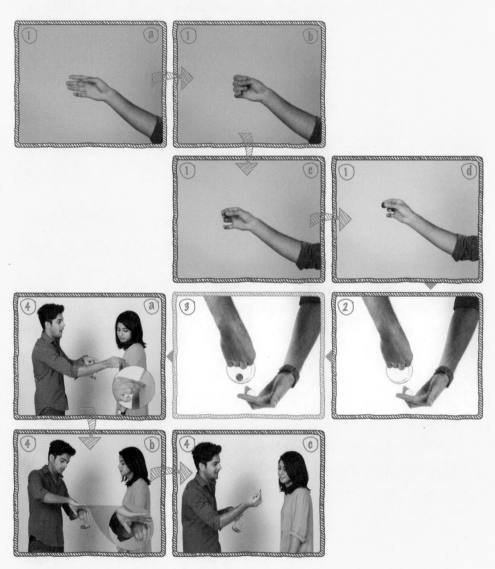

Neel's Tip: *Move 3 might require some practice.*

The Classic Palm Technique is most commonly employed in coin magic. This is a skill—facilitated by keeping the fingers free for movement—by which the magician can hold a coin in their hand but impress upon the spectator that their hand is empty.

1. Hold the coin with your thumb on one side and your ring and index fingers on the other. At this stage, the coin is visible to the spectator.

2. Curl in your ring and index fingers, and press the coin to the centre of your palm. This can be done on the sly when your hand is pointing downwards.

3. Now grip the coin with the help of the muscles of the palm.

4. Your fingers can function freely—they can move and pick up objects—as only your palm clenches the hidden coin.

Money has always been an object of desire for man. The fact that a piece of metal could buy anything gave it an esteemed status, which people often associated with magical power. In Central Europe, people believed in a mysterious coin called the inkluz. The magical aspect of this coin was that it would always come back to the owner, upon one condition. If the owner remembered to collect change from every transaction that they made, the inkluz would someday come back to them, in their pocket or purse. The inkluz is supposed to look strikingly different, so that it is not confused with other ordinary coins. However, if the owner forgot the rule, it would never return to them again.

Legends of the magical coin have been prevalent in many parts of Europe since the 10th century. And a lot of these tales developed around coins that were of foreign origins, were inscribed with strange characters and drawings, and looked mysterious.

Out of the Box

I was seventeen, still in boarding school, when I encountered an incident that showed grit, determination and, well, style.

The inter-house athletics competition—or the Athletics Comp, as it was known—was one of the main sporting events at Doon in which the entire school would participate. And when I say the whole school, I mean all 500 of us! I used to take part in the high jump contest and the 200-metre race. I even represented my school in the Dehradun district championships—so I guess I was pretty decent. But we all had to practise like there was no tomorrow. And once in a while, Doon School would discover a legend— someone who was good at everything. And with that, came that once-in-a-lifetime high as all the boys shouted, cheered and applauded them for being a champion. But this story is not about the legend.

During one such Athletics Comp, all the participants were getting ready for the 5000-metre race. They had lined up with their foot on the line, one of which belonged to my friend.

Let me tell you something about my friend. He used to be really overweight and, one day, he decided to shed it all. That boy had great resolve. Wearing layers and layers of sweaters to sweat it out, he would run—starting off slow but gradually increasing the number of rounds. He also took care of his diet with extreme discipline, except for Tuesdays. Because, on Tuesdays, the Central Dining Hall—the CDH—was kind enough to serve us pasta. For us boarders, that was a treat—even if it wasn't the best-tasting pasta.

It was palatable enough. And so, every Tuesday, my friend and I would sit together at the same table in the CDH for dinner, to eat heartily and have a good conversation over a bowl of pasta.

But now my friend stood lined up for the final Athletics Comp showdown—the 5000-metre race. The whistle was blown and the participants took off. And I saw that all the athletes were racing at a considerable speed, except for my friend, who was somewhat jogging! A trio of potential winners took the lead from the rest of the athletes, while bringing up the rear was our unlikely hero. He was slow, excruciatingly slow. Clearly my friend had a lot of catching up to do, but he just kept going at his leisurely pace.

He was doing his rounds in slo-mo, a unique and innovative style. The front runners caught up with him again and again as they completed the rounds swiftly, and then one final time to finish the race amidst thunderous cheering. While everyone was busy reaching the finishing line, my friend—in his slo-mo fashion—was just on his fourth round with eight more to go!

Slowly, the crowd started dissipating, but he kept going. He kept running. Round after round, he kept getting closer to his target. And by the time he had just four rounds left, the word spread and people started returning to the field to watch my friend as he was still running without giving up.

But even *he* hadn't anticipated what happened next! By the time he started his last lap, the whole school had landed up to cheer for my friend who was running his lone battle. Now everyone gave him a reason to finish the race. They were cheering his name, some kids were even running along with him to give him moral support. Then a miracle happened. My friend finally broke into a sprint and ran the whole way, right till the finishing line! The students applauded him wildly. All in all, he finished the race in absolute style.

Coincidentally, that day turned out to be a Tuesday—and you know what that means, don't you? We ate like wild beasts. Even the pasta tasted better than usual!

A boarder's life is a vastly different affair from a day scholar's. Our dorms were our second home and our friends, more than family. And everyone's birthday was like our own!

Thus, each and every boy's birthday was a special occasion, celebrated in the house or at the housemaster's residence. And there was *so* much excitement associated with the event. Come to think of it now, we made such a hullabaloo about nothing! We left no stone unturned in ensuring that the young lad had a great day by whatever means. On the eve of a birthday, we'd be huddled in complete darkness around the birthday boy's bed at midnight to celebrate with candles and torchlights.

On the particular night that I can recall fondly, a kid had recently got some money and tuck from his visit home, and he was yet to deposit it with the housemaster. The money was still lying in his drawer and I asked him if I could use some of it. The junior was initially pretty taken aback by my plea. But, later, my magic tricks turned the element of shock into a happy surprise!

At this point, my dorm-mates—the senior boys—were attacking the tuck, while I kept the younger lads engaged with a magic stunt. These young fellows were so distracted that they did not notice, till much later, that their tuck had been raided clean by the seniors.

The trick that I performed for them—plucking currency notes out of thin air—happens to be quite easy. It also gives people the illusion of getting hold of money—a thing that attracts everyone's attention, whatever their age. Especially if you have no money to speak of!

make It Rain

Producing a stack of notes from thin air

> **MATERIAL REQUIRED:**
> A stack of ten to twelve crisp banknotes.

PREPARATION: Place the spectator directly in front of you. It is essential to wear a long-sleeved shirt that is quite loose-fitting. Before starting the trick, roll up the stack of notes tightly and place them in the bend of either of your arms, well concealed by the folds of your shirt. Your gimmick is ready!

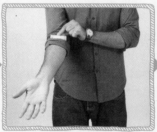

THE TRICK DECODED

① Begin the trick by showing your audience that both your hands are completely empty. You could also jokingly lift up a bit of your sleeves to make them believe that there's nothing fishy going on!

② Now pretend to roll up your sleeves to give the impression that you are preparing for the trick! However, while you do it, discreetly retrieve the stack of notes from the bend of your arm and hold them tightly in your fist.

③ Clasp both your hands together and with a vigorous rubbing motion, proceed to spew a fountain of bills—seemingly out of nowhere!

Neel's Tip: *You have to be extremely careful about the placement of the bundle of notes in the crook of your arm. You must also be adept at the process of pulling out the notes from there and stuffing them in your fist. It goes without saying that this trick requires ample practice even though it might seem easy at first.*

School was probably the best five years of my life. As you can see, it was just one crazy roller-coaster ride. And the Doon School really had its own charm.

Often we'd still be running on the pebbled path under the shade of the trees when we'd hear the second bell ringing, which meant that the classes had begun and that we were late. Then the teacher would mark us late on their computer screen, also giving us a complimentary punishment known as a dirty gab or DG. But if the teacher was in a good mood, we would try to get our A-game on in convincing them not to mark us late. Basically, we never wanted to get marked late because that meant that we wouldn't be able to do a few things that we'd ideally like to do—such as having money for the tuck shop, getting phone chits and other allowances. Thus, whenever the bell rang, everyone would run for their lives and make sure that at least one part of their body was inside the classroom before the sound of the last bell rang out!

As I moved on to the twelfth standard, I was beginning to find more and more joy in toying around with random objects after class hours, and finding ways to change their shape, size and form. Or just getting them to vanish altogether! Anything and everything would catch my fancy—all that mattered was their availability in my immediate vicinity. I have to admit that all my form-mates were always encouraging of my fascinating hobby, for, sometimes, it even saved us from some real trouble.

It was a Thursday evening, and four of my dorm-mates had decided to 'bust bounds'—a term that we used for jumping the school boundary wall and going into town, without the permission of the housemaster. But I must say, these rather adventurous outings came with their share of trepidation and the danger of getting caught. This is because these activities invited rather harsh punishment, including suspension from school. But such is teenage life! You want to do things that are experimental, knowing full well that you can get into trouble for them. Busting bounds was mostly attempted just for the fun of it and to get food from town to satisfy the hunger pangs of teenage boys for whom no amount of food is sufficient.

On that evening, suddenly a junior came running to us, to announce that the housemaster was walking towards our Toye room. With four of our friends absent, we had to think quickly. Out came a secret phone to inform our friends in town that danger loomed close. And to buy some time, I was asked to rustle up an impromptu show in a minute. That is how I got to do my first 'live show' and it lasted a good half an hour.

I recall accosting them—my housemaster and another teacher who accompanied him—in the veranda. A few initial tricks aroused interest and I moved on to more intricate illusions. And they both got into the mood for a show! Some juniors brought in a few chairs and the veranda became the venue of my first live performance at the young age of seventeen. Several other students peered out of their Toye room too. I carried on with my show, while keeping my eyes peeled for my four runaway pals.

Just as I was growing afraid that I would exhaust my repertoire of magic tricks, the four young lads waved from the far end of the corridor! They had made their way back to the Toye room. Show time was over. The housemaster even complimented me and asked me to pay as much attention to my studies as I did to magic! This evoked laughter all around—especially from the other teacher.

An interesting feature of school life is managing the egos of seniors, while staying on the straight and narrow path—which, simply put, translates into 'staying out of trouble'! We all know that the teenage years can be fairly volatile. While the school authorities and masters do keep a check, largely exerting control, the boys have to navigate unknown terrains on their own.

A friend of mine and I were perpetually in trouble with the seniors. The implications of such a scenario are straightforward—either suffer the punishment or find a way out. And find a way out we did. One has to use one's persuasive skills as well as some other not-so-legal skills to avoid getting in a fix.

For instance, I had a passion for doodling and calligraphy, and, as part of that project, I could copy the signatures of various masters. One day, one of my seniors saw me scribbling and immediately ordered me to forge the housemaster's signature on the 'bad chit' in his notebook. A bad chit was part of a regular process in which a note was issued by the subject teacher and had to be shown to the housemaster who would then sign off on it.

All of a sudden, the process became simpler—no standing in line, no admonishment from the housemaster and no guilt. There was an alternative that had come into play. Most of the seniors started making a beeline for me to get the housemaster's signature on their bad chits. I was in great demand, and getting bossed around by seniors was a thing of the past.

This skill, combined with my magical abilities, helped me to gain many friends who were senior to me—a rare occurrence in the fairly hierarchical boarding school structure. And, even today, several of them are still my friends even though we're now well past school life.

Studies, of course, *were* the most integral part of our school life and large chunks of our morning and evening hours were dedicated to them. One winter afternoon right before the exams, in my final year at school, we were sitting in the stone corridor desperately longing for the sun to shine through the cloudy sky. Just then, I saw Vicky, the sweeper boy, pass by. He wasn't exactly a peculiar-looking guy, except for a tuft of hair falling on his forehead which was mostly kept in place by oodles and oodles of oil. Another noticeable thing about him was the bunch of rings that he wore on his fingers, making him look like an astrologer's delight.

New as I still was in trying to create tricks, the multitude of fancy rings on Vicky's fingers caught my attention. I walked up to the young man and asked if I could borrow a ring that was inexpensive. And just as he took off his ring, the sun shone from behind the clouds, the rays catching the surface of the artificial silver. A glint, a sparkle! Or did the ring wink at me, trying to tell me something?

Eureka! Got it!

Ring of Illusion

Creating the effect of a solid ring passing right through a finger

> **MATERIAL REQUIRED:**
> One ring.

PREPARATION: Make sure that the ring you choose fits quite loosely around your little finger so that it can come off in a flash.

THE TRICK DECODED

① Place the spectator directly in front of you. Stretch your palm out to them—with the ring worn loosely around the tip of your little finger—in their line of vision in such a way that your little finger faces them.

② Push the ring almost all the way down around your little finger.

③ Tell the spectator to focus on the ring. Now swiftly remove the ring from the finger and bring the ring exactly in front of it!

Neel's Tip: *The trick is extremely simple but requires practice to make the execution neat, and create the illusion of the ring passing through your finger.*

It may have become apparent by now that I wasn't a born nerd. One day during Toye time, my chemistry teacher—whom we called MLB—walked in to supervise us. That day, I was in no mood to bury my nose in a book and learn the complicated combinations of chemistry—a subject that, frankly, I found the most useless of all.

As MLB approached me, I stood up and suddenly called out to her, 'Ma'am, look there, look there!' pointing down at nothing in particular on the floor. MLB, of course, was taken aback, and reacted immediately by looking in the direction I was pointing at with my left hand. And, taking advantage of the situation, I sneakily dropped a card into the pocket of her overcoat with my other hand.

A young lad behind me called out rather cheekily. 'Bravo!'

And that's when the real magic began—Toye time was forgotten because of my prank, much to the delight of all who were around. All were in a mood for fun!

But I have to add that, in retrospect, I wish I had spent more time studying chemistry and physics. Simply because they are the most useful subjects of all, especially to a magician!

Cups and Balls

Making balls pass through cups

MATERIAL REQUIRED:
Three identical cups and four identical small-sized balls. Crumpled tissues or cloth balls can also be used. Ensure that the material used is soft so that the secret ball does not make any noise when the cups are upturned. Do not use balls made of rubber as they can be bouncy!

For easy understanding, let's name the cups 1, 2 and 3. And let's call the balls A, B, C and D.

PREPARATION: Before starting the trick, stack two of the cups together. The lowest cup is cup 1 and the cup above it is cup 2. Place one ball—ball A—inside cup 2 and hide the ball by placing cup 3 on top.

THE TRICK DECODED

① Put the three remaining balls—B, C and D—on the table, in a row but separated with gaps between them.

② Place one upturned cup behind each ball. Cup 2, with the secret ball, goes in the centre. Practise this many times to make sure that the hidden ball does not fall out! To ensure this, flip the cup very swiftly. Tap each of the three cups with a pencil—or a wand—to prove to the spectator that they are empty.

③ Place the ball that you put in the centre—ball B—on top of cup 2, which is behind it.

④ Stack the other two cups—cups 1 and 3—on top of ball B.

⑤ Tap the topmost cup (cup 3) in the stack with your pencil or wand, and then lift all three cups together to show that the ball has gone through! The spectator will think that this is ball B, but this is actually the secret ball A.

⑥ Shuffle the stack, making cup 1 the bottommost. Show the spectator that it covers ball A, but it also has ball B inside it (from step 3) that the audience doesn't see because of the swift flip.

⑦ Place ball C on top of cup 1, which has balls A and B underneath it, and stack cups 2 and 3 on top of it.

⑧ Tap the topmost cup (cup 2) with your pencil or wand, and then lift all three cups together to show that another ball—two now—has gone through the cup! For this, release the ball that you had placed in step 3 (ball B), though the spectator will think it is the ball you'd placed on top of the cup (ball C) in step 7.

⑨ Shuffle the stack, making cup 3 the bottommost. Show the spectator that it covers balls A and B, but it also has ball C inside it (from step 7) that the audience doesn't see because of the swift flip.

⑩ Place the fourth and last ball (ball D) on top of cup 3, which has three balls (A, B and C) underneath it. Stack the other two cups on top of it.

⑪ Once again, tap the topmost cup (cup 1) with your pencil or wand and lift all three cups together to show that another ball—three now—has gone through the cup! For this, release the ball that you had placed in step 7 (ball C), though the spectator will think it is the ball you'd placed on top of the cup (ball D) in step 10.

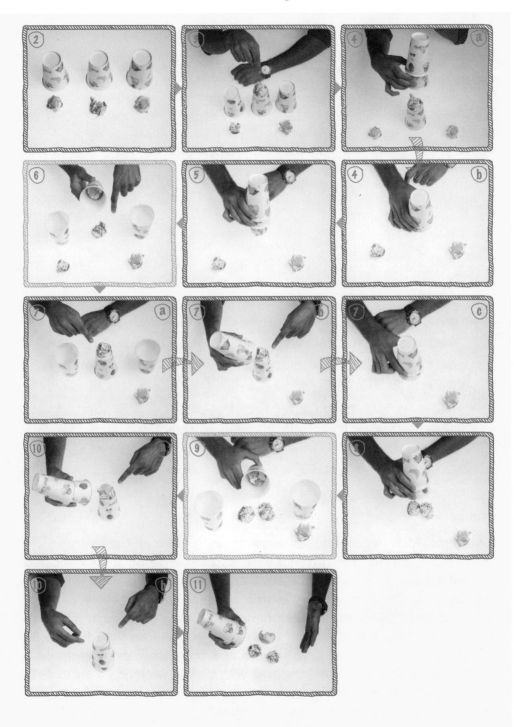

Neel's Tip:

- *Although there are three cups and four balls at play, the spectator should only know of three cups and three balls.*

- *The crux of this trick lies in being clean and swift when turning the cup with the secret ball. While doing so, the cup should be placed on the surface before the ball falls out.*

- *While performing this trick, keep talking to the spectator to distract them, so that they do not watch your hands closely. Tell them a funny story—to make them look at you instead. The spectator will tend to look at what you are looking at. So, if you are constantly watching your 'dirty work', the audience will most likely watch it as well! A good method of distraction is to not look at what you don't want the spectator to see. Practise the movements of the trick enough, so that you don't need to watch what you are doing in order to perform it.*

Mastering a cups-and-balls routine will mean that one has mastered most of the fundamental techniques of magic. The gimmick includes vanishing, appearing, transpositions and substitutions. Basic but crucial skills like the placement of the audience, dexterity of movement and misdirection are essential to a cups-and-balls trick. Grasping the aptitude for this trick is considered a formal benchmark for a magician. The revered king of magic, Harry Houdini, believed that no one could be considered a proficient magician until they had become proficient with cups and balls.

Over time, MLB became quite special to us. And I look back very fondly upon an incident during my final year at Doon. Five of us had decided to bust bounds in order to take advantage of a discount at our favourite restaurant at Hotel President—a free paneer dish with every plate of butter chicken! It was also another matter that I hadn't ever busted bounds before, and I wanted to tick off that experience before I graduated. So off we went—a group of four fit boys and one rather overweight one. While the four of us jumped the wall with agility, we made sure to help our struggling friend over as well. A run to the restaurant added to the excitement, making us very ravenous indeed! Soon we were ensconced in a quiet area of the restaurant. As we were digging into our food twenty minutes later, in walked MLB with her husband! And she was guided to the table right next to us. None of us knew what to do. Should we run or should we stay?

She looked at us, and we looked back at her. Then we looked at the table laid with food! Keeping a straight face, we greeted her and went back to dinner, as if we had done no wrong. When we returned to school, we were sure that we would be in trouble but—can you believe it—MLB did not sneak! The above encounter taught me a lesson—*don't run when you are not being chased!* And it's an important lesson in life as well as magic.

The next time in the chemistry laboratory, I was once again aiming to lighten the mood with my tricks, for this subject seemed too boring to me. What was I going to achieve by learning all the formulae, I used to think. MLB looked at me and looked away, nodding her head. I wondered if she had forgiven me for playing tricks on her in the Toye room and for busting bounds. It seemed she had, for she smiled at me—and I smiled back, albeit naughtily. For I was already thinking of another trick! This time, with some spare coins in my pocket.

The Coin's Watching You

A coin passes through the bottom of a glass

MATERIAL REQUIRED:
One empty, transparent glass, one pen and a signed coin.

THE TRICK DECODED

① Ask the spectator for a coin, which they should sign and give to you.

② Hold the glass in your left hand and place the coin under the bottom of the glass.

③ Tap the coin against the base twice. This will show the spectator that you're trying to push the coin through the bottom of the glass.

④ On the third time, swiftly slam it. But, this time, bring the coin to your fingertip and dunk it into the glass. This needs to be done right after the second tap so that the spectator cannot discern the swiftness of the move.

⑤ Hand the glass to them so that they can inspect it.

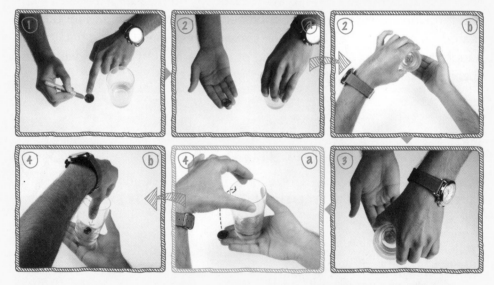

Neel's Tip: *This trick requires a little practice, but is a sure-shot method of dazzling crowds at parties!*

School was supposed to shut for the annual winter break with the kids going back home for the vacations. But, before that, we *had* to play our final inter-school football match, since, as I've mentioned, sports was one of the most loved activities for all of us. I used to love football—indeed, one could interchange the word 'love' with 'madness'. I wish there was an even stronger word for my passion! I was also part of the school team. The thrill of playing against another team, the desire to pit ourselves against an equally avid opponent, the zeal to win, the determination to outdo everyone else—all this would energize and propel us to do our best.

Our last match before school broke up for the holidays was a more special affair than the rest because, unlike most times when we would play against the Welham Boys or the Mayo Boys, this time, a match was due with a boys' school from Haryana. And boy, those lanky fellows from the plains seemed to have it in them—that seething fire in their belly that made their thirst to win a rather primal affair. But we Doscos were confident that we were made of sterner stuff and had the requisite skills.

On the D-Day, oddly enough, this match didn't turn out like the rest, contrary to our confidence. Nobody saw it coming—their victory and our loss. Although we scored first, the Haryana boys played tough and used rough tackles, got dirtier than us, looked grittier than us and scored twice in the second half. What can I say, victory was well and truly theirs! While it was disconcerting to lose on home ground, we couldn't do much except accept the results and try to work harder the next time around.

The already darkened skies seemed more gloomy as each one of us sat nursing a bruised ego. But a senior made us respect the opposition's win—that they passed the ball better, had long-range shooting skills, and their forwards had the speed to test our defence time and again. If our goalkeeper hadn't saved a couple of their other brilliant long-range shots with great diving saves, the difference in score would have been even worse for us.

While everyone still looked disappointed, and were exhausted and thirsty, I decided to attempt to lift the pall of gloom and lighten everyone's spirits. So, as we all made our way to the CDH for something to drink, I caught sight of a knife and some bread.

And it worked! Magic had the last word. As was expected, the team looked brighter, the tiredness ebbed away and excitement crept in as we were all set to go home the next morning.

Knife from Nowhere

A knife magically comes out of a loaf of bread

> **MATERIAL REQUIRED:**
> One loaf of bread—preferably a baguette—and a butter knife. Ensure that the baguette is bigger than the size of the knife.

PREPARATION: **Place the spectator directly in front of you. When no one's looking, take the knife and hold it under your right forearm. Hold the handle of the knife with your middle, ring and little fingers. Turn your hand and rest it on the table to conceal the knife from the spectator until you start the trick.**

THE TRICK DECODED

1. Hold the baguette carefully with your left hand and bring it to the top of your forearm, where the knife is concealed.

2. Once you're sure that the view of your right forearm is not visible to the spectator, turn your arm around—immediately placing the tip of the knife under the baguette.

3. Pin the knife with the fingers of your left hand. Now you're holding the knife and the baguette in the same grip; your right hand is free.

④ Press the baguette on to the tip of the knife with your left hand.

⑤ Once the tip of the knife pierces the baguette, slowly insert the knife into the baguette lengthwise. This should be done with the fingers of your left hand, on the underside of the baguette. If needed, you can also use your right hand to hold the baguette. This is when you need to distract the spectator from what your hands are doing.

⑥ Once the insertion is done, bend the baguette from the middle. This position will reveal the knife after a while. Start pulling out the knife with your bare hands.

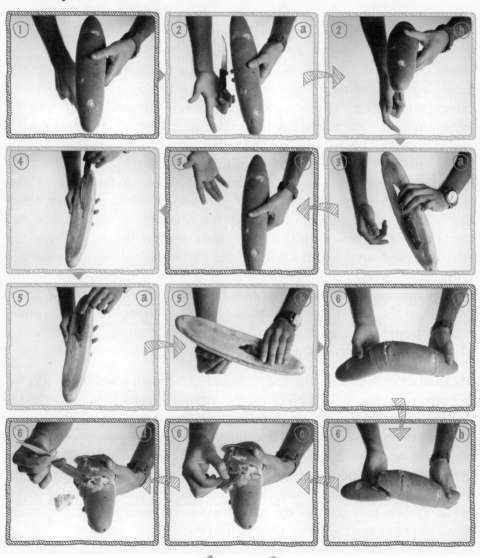

Neel's Tip: *Although the images show the use of a serrated knife—for safety purposes, you can also use a butter knife. This trick is a combination of a thorough set-up as well as theatrics. Once you have placed the knife under the loaf of bread, the trick lies in distracting your spectator by engaging them in conversation.*

School shut for the annual winter break—my last one before I graduated—and I went off home. Schools in the hills, as most of you know, close for a good three months when the higher reaches of north India are flushed with snow, when chilly winds make it too harsh for young boarders to stay on.

Christmas back home is usually a massive affair. Family, friends, young and old cousins, grandparents, aunts, uncles and a whole barrage of other sundry relatives converge. At least that's how it works in India—no family event is devoid of togetherness. This particular Christmas, my parents and I decided to head to Almora along with our uncle, a very close family friend from London. Neither a village nor a town—Almora is a small, sleepy locale up in the Kumaon Himalayas. Uncle, as part of his charity work, was supporting a particular school called Gandhi Ashram near Almora. His contribution was special for it was not just money, but time, effort and lots of love for all the girls who attended the school. In fact, he was a bit like Santa Claus, bringing laughter, warmth and presents, of course, for all the kids of Gandhi Ashram. And for three whole days, we accompanied Uncle and spent time with the young girls who continued to live in the school throughout the cold winter, taking part in various workshops. It was particularly freezing there because there was no electricity to keep the heaters running, as the electric poles had fallen down due to the heavy snow. And the Christmas holidays prevented the electricity department workers from fixing the situation. But that did not dampen the enthusiasm of the young students of Gandhi Ashram.

My mother also pitched in and conducted a theatre workshop on the importance of the girl child, using the interplay of local Kumaoni songs and the Kumaoni dialect. Uncle mimed a hilarious comedy show, playing a village dentist, even getting a couple of the village folk to participate. My father, who was also with us, was the one clicking all the photographs. I, of course, had been assigned the task of performing a magic show on Christmas Day. I spent the entire day with the young schoolchildren, teaching them only some of the basic tricks using coins and rubber bands, as we did not have too much time to ourselves.

In the winter afternoon on the day of the Christmas show, the celebrations were further warmed by the presence of the many people from the village who had come to help. The school teachers were putting up a small stage while some young girls were serving coffee and tea in thermocol glasses. Despite the crippling cold, the bustle and excitement were palpable. As some kids were busy practising drama, some dancing, some just sitting around and chatting—my curious eyes were fixed on those thermocol glasses.

I picked one up and observed its specifications carefully—the dimensions, the weight, the size. All of it.

And about half an hour later, a few young students were staring in awe at one of the glasses hanging in mid-air between my hands. I smiled and decided to decode it for them.

Cup Up and Away!

A cup floats in mid-air between the magician's palms

MATERIAL REQUIRED:
An opaque styrofoam cup. You can also use an opaque paper cup.

PREPARATION: Pierce a hole with your thumb on the side of the cup that faces you. Push your thumb into this hole slightly to get a grip to hold on to the cup. To make it more impactful, leave a bit of a drink in the cup and keep sipping it in the middle of the trick!

THE TRICK DECODED

1. With your thumb crammed into the back of the cup, place the other thumb behind the cup. This should give you a firm hold.

2. Now extend and gently release all the other fingers at the same time to give the effect that you are letting go of the cup and that it is now floating.

3. To make it look like its floating forward, move your fingers forward!

Neel's Tip: *Always remember that the back of the cup, along with your thumb, should be hidden from the spectator. It's important to make it look like the cup has a mind of its own, and that you're just trying to control it so that it doesn't escape!*

Many legends from all over the world talk about sages and extraordinary men who attempted things that are ordinarily beyond the capacity of humans. One such man was Abraham Ibn Ezra, a very popular figure in Jewish folklore from the Middle Ages. Apart from being a revered poet and a philosopher, he's known as the rescuer of Jews who stood up against the harsh dictums of the rulers. The magical element about him was the duality of his character. He could apparently make himself invisible, pass through solid walls and perform miracles. It is said that he was a magical wanderer who would stay at a place for a brief time and then disappear into thin air.

It was the end of December and we made our way to Delhi. While still enjoying the winter vacations, I was due to visit my grandparents there over the period of New Year's. I was really excited about the visit since we hadn't seen each other in a while! My nani loved me a lot and doted on me wholly. In fact, as soon as we reached Delhi, she invited all us cousins to her house and treated us to our favourite dishes. Dal makhani with lots of home-made white, unsalted butter was right on top of that list! By evening, we had gathered around a bonfire that had been readied on the lawn, as per the yearly winter ritual—which, I reckon, is a feature in most north Indian homes.

My nana had a really old ink pen that his father had given him as a prize for becoming an officer in the Indian Army way back in the early 1950s. This prized object had its origins in Germany and wore a stunning peacock-blue armour with a silver rim. It looked so regal!

Nana had discerned that his favourite grandkid had had his eyes set on the pen for ages at this point. As a kid, I was always the quiet one before the strict family patriarch, and could never gather the guts to ask for the pen—let alone ever dream of owning it. But thanks to the magical antics that I'd been engaging in at Doon—and with a certain calculated thought in my head—I confidently walked up to Nana and asked for a banknote. Very lovingly, he pulled out a crisp bill from his leather wallet and handed it to me.

The next thing I did was ask for his pen! This time, too, I was met with the same response, albeit with a frown. With pursed lips that were accompanied with the stern look of an army officer, the article was pulled out from the pocket of his blazer. But suddenly, I saw that the eyes were warm, fixed at me. Nana seemed to be smiling behind his moustache.

No one in the family had ever imagined me doing this, but I still went ahead with—guess what—a trick! My hands were in action and the bill was in mid-air with the shiny, ancient blue pen passing through it.

How did that happen? How could *such a thing happen?* Nobody knew, and everybody wondered with their mouths hanging open in pure stupefaction! A collective 'WOW!' emanated from the crowd.

Everybody rushed to grab the banknote and the pen to inspect them for any loopholes, passing them from hand to hand till they finally reached my nana. The excitement was electric, and I was heartily congratulated and patted on the back with some rather heavy hands. Lots of backslapping! From the quiet one, I was suddenly the star kid in the family!

And then the inevitable happened. I felt a tap on my back amidst all the loud cheers. As I turned around, I saw my dear old nana standing and smiling a most contented and proud smile. The crow's feet around his eyes deepened as he smiled at me that warm smile. The glint in his eyes said it all. He extended his hand and there it was, the legendary blue pen!

Handing it over to me, he said, 'Go ahead, Neel. Write more magical tales with it!'

'Nana! How can I take it from you?' Then quickly, without waiting for an answer, I grabbed the pen and pocketed it, politely adding, 'Oh! Thank you, Nana!'

'Not at all!' My grandfather hollered.

In the cacophony of cheers, a loud voice yelled from somewhere, 'Hey, Neel! Go patent your stories. You've got magic!'

I was the proud owner of a legacy now. Not just a beautiful blue pen, but also a name.

You Got Magic.

At that time, though, I wondered where I would use that name. I hadn't the faintest idea!

Pen Pierces the Note

A pen passes through the middle of a banknote

> **MATERIAL REQUIRED:**
> One banknote, and a pen or pencil.

PREPARATION: Before starting the trick, make a small and neat cut in the note, close to one of its narrower lengths. Make sure that the slit is made in an area which is dark in colour and that it is big enough for the pen to pass through. The slit should be neat and tiny so that it does not catch the spectator's attention.

THE TRICK DECODED

① With the spectator directly in front of you, fold the note in half, lengthwise.

② Insert and pass your pen through the slit without actually making it go through the centre-fold of the note.

③ Show the note to the spectator from one side, which will lead them to believe that the pen has completely pierced the folded note.

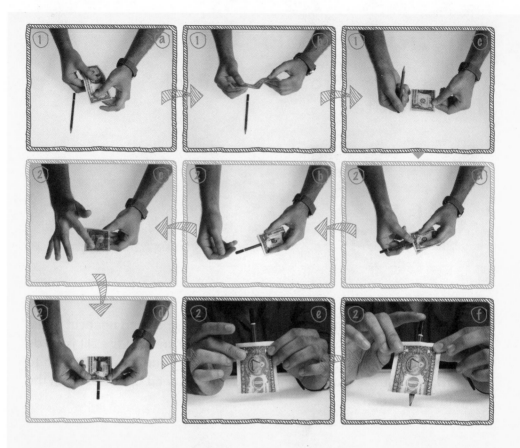

Neel's Tip: *This trick requires your spectator to be sitting at an angle from which they cannot see the slit in the note. When I did this trick for the first time in front of my nana, I'd just got his pen and a banknote in front of the whole family. I turned away from the gathering to quickly set my trick up, and made a slit in the note. The spontaneity of the trick added to the effect. Simple as it may seem, this trick requires a lot of practice!*

The Moment of a Lifetime— The First of Many

What does an eighteen-year-old do in New York, especially after six years of a relatively simple life in a boarding school, back when a trekking trip was the highlight of his teenage life? I know what most eighteen-year-olds would do immediately after descending on the bustling streets of Manhattan. I, too, started the same way—jumping right in to explore the city. But along the road, I began to feel the need to introspect.

Do eighteen-year-olds introspect, you ask? Yes, they do!

It was the summer of 2011, I had finished my schooling in India and was travelling to the United States to figure out my future prospects. My mother and I had New York and Boston marked on our agenda. My father, a senior media industry professional, was at Harvard Business School in Boston, attending the Advanced Management Program. While he studied at the age of fifty, I had the opportunity to consider the option of pursuing my undergraduate studies in the US. My objective was to try and find a programme that would be of interest to me and, towards this end, I started exploring colleges and universities in the city of Boston.

And as soon as I stepped inside the gates of an American university, namely Boston University, I was bowled over! I was greeted by well-manicured lawns, imposing buildings, huge libraries, warm and helpful professors, bustling corridors, spacious classrooms and, of course, a plethora of students of all nationalities. The sight of the sheer number of students dashing to their lectures, always so busy, was also quite overwhelming.

Just then, I stopped to think to myself—*is this where I want to spend the next four years of my life?* And thus started the introspection as well as the comparisons.

Back home in India, most major universities accept students purely on the basis of a few digits on paper i.e., marks. But American universities invite broader applications that test not only your textbook understanding but also the overall depth of your thought and knowledge. And this distinction really stood out for me, for I never was inclined towards rote learning.

I wasn't a nerd by any measure. And I could adjust to the idea of living away from my family, even be okay with missing home-cooked food. But the one element of my life that I was not going to compromise on was my private, quiet time. These were moments that I spent away from my peers and peer pressure, away from food and foodies, away from cafes and nightclubs, away from shops and shopaholics. This was a time that was entirely mine to explore and I found it the most magical. It was a personal perspective on creating magic that I had developed as I had grown out of my boyhood years.

Magic, I believe, comes from silence—because each person can appreciate magic in their own way. For every single person, the same piece of magic is different. And as an illusionist—I was beginning to learn—it was my job to make the spectator feel that way about magic. And if I didn't, then I was doing magic wrong. I needed to figure out how to make the spectator not even *want* to catch me out. I needed to figure out how they would agree to put their guard down so that I could perform my best for them.

As I sat in a cafe at BU, I noticed that there was no silence in the vibrant city life—the place was bursting with activity and everyone was just so busy. And while I was lounging about with some new friends I'd just made, I shared two tricks with the students attending the university. Two tricks which broke all cultural barriers. And it was my instinct, at that moment of performance, which helped me make up my mind.

Without a Trace

A card held in the magician's hand vanishes into thin air while their open palm can be seen to be completely empty

> MATERIAL REQUIRED:
> One playing card.

THE TRICK DECODED

1. Hold a card lengthwise with your thumb on one plane and your index, middle and ring fingers on the other.

2. Now use your index and little fingers to tightly grip the corners of the narrower edge of the card. And curl in your middle and ring fingers against the back plane of the card.

3. Now uncurl the middle and ring fingers. This will bring the card round to the other side—the back—of the hand.

4. You card has vanished from the spectator's view!

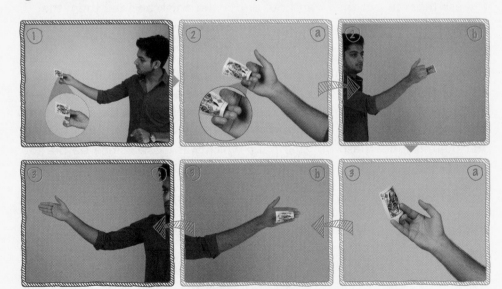

Neel's Tip: *Even though this trick seems immensely easy, needless to say, it requires a lot of practice. Make sure that you've mastered the movement in front of the mirror a good number of times before you show it to someone else. This trick also requires the spectator to stand directly in front of you, so that they are unable to see the back of your hand i.e., where the card will reappear.*

Are you well versed with the suits in a deck of cards? Do you know what each of the four suits represents? Interestingly, a deck of cards carries imprints of the four major strata of the Middle Ages. The hearts represent the Church, clubs represent agriculture, spades represent the military and diamonds represent the merchant class.

Another illusion I performed at the cafe is one trick to attempt when you're trying to break the ice. To date, it is one of my favourite ways to strike up a conversation with someone for the first time—while also trying to impress them with a few skills up my sleeve!

For instance, if you go up to someone and tell them that both of you are connected, they won't believe you at first. But you can *get* them to believe you by telling them that you will prove it. So how *can* you prove it?

You ask them to put their hand out and make a fist, and tell them that if, in fact, the two of you *are* linked, then whatever happens to you should happen to them as well. Let's hope they agree.

Then you take some ash and put it on your palm. Start rubbing the mark on your palm and, very soon, the ash will disappear. Then you can claim that if you put ash on your hand, technically, there should be ash on their hand as well! And if you ask them to open their hand, then they will see that there is indeed ash on their palm which was closed since before the trick started.

Another version of this incredible illusion is perhaps easier to start with.

A Surprise Tattoo

The magician asks the spectator to select a card. Without looking at it, the magician reveals that the spectator's chosen card has been stamped with ash across their forearm

> **MATERIAL REQUIRED:**
> A deck of playing cards, a tube or tin of chapstick, a pencil, a scrap of paper, an ashtray and a lighter.

PREPARATION: **Choose a card and place it at the bottom of the deck. Let us use the Ace of Hearts as an example. Prepare your arm by writing the card's name on your forearm with the chapstick. Your gimmick is ready!**

THE TRICK DECODED

① You'll begin your trick with a technique called the Criss-Cross Force.

   ⓐ Set the deck on the table face down. Tell the spectator to cut the deck at any point.

   ⓑ Pick up the bottom half of the deck with your right hand and tell the spectator that you're about to mark the point at which the spectator had cut the deck.

   ⓒ Place the portion of the deck with the chosen card—held in your right hand—on top of the remaining half of the deck, thus forming a cross.

   ⓓ Now show them the bottommost card of the top portion of the deck and tell them that this is the card that they had selected. Show it to them in such a way that there's no way for you to see the card. You're actually showing the spectator the bottommost card of the deck—the Ace of Hearts that you placed—but due to the cross formation, they'll think that it's the card from the middle of the deck, at exactly the point where they cut it!

② Ask the spectator to remember the card and keep the deck aside.

③ Turn around and tell the spectator to write the name of the card—that they had selected and were shown—on a piece of paper. Once the spectator has done so, tell them to fold the paper as many times as they want. Take the paper from them and burn it in front of them.

④ Collect all the ash in the ashtray and allow it some time to cool down.

⑤ Pick up the flakes of ash and rub them generously on your forearm. Then allow the chapstick to do its magic. The ashes stick to your arm and the name of the selected card appears imprinted on it!

Playing cards is one of the most popular activities in any social gathering. Have you ever wondered where the cards originated? The first reference to playing cards was found back in 1120 AD in an ancient Chinese dictionary. They were invented in the court of Seun-Ho who used them for his entertainment and the amusement of his numerous concubines.

After exploring several universities, I went to New York to spend time with my aunt and uncle, where they lived in a beautiful home in the Upper West Side. While in New York City, I undertook explorations typical of a tourist. Times Square was fascinating at night; bright lights dominated the mindscape from every possible angle. The same could be said for Central Park in the daytime—every walkway had a clear view of the sunlight streaming from behind the skyline. The Brooklyn Bridge was overpowering; a Broadway musical left me spellbound. The smell of freshly ground coffee wafted through the air from the cafes along Broadway. And there were the shops along Fifth Avenue which, well, emptied my pockets. The quintessential yellow cab, and its driver—commonly from India or Pakistan—allowed me the rare pleasure of speaking in my own native language while I was lost in the soul-city of the United States of America. I flew aloft with the sheer energy of Manhattan, enjoying every bit of my sojourn, meeting plenty of old and new friends. The pace was truly infectious!

After a few heady weeks, I wished to find quiet spots in Manhattan. I found the Conservatory Garden—a beautiful enclosure of three smaller gardens on the east side of Central Park between 103rd Street and 106th Street. They are quieter than the south end of Central Park, less frequented by tourists and great places for relaxation and reflection.

Pointing me to a similar location, my aunt suggested a trip to the Gantry Plaza State Park on Long Island. So one morning I donned my jacket, ready to leave for the park, which was some distance away, in search of a serene spot. Just then, my aunt added with a chuckle and a glint in her naughty eyes, 'Neel, Bollywood movies often shoot their dance sequences there as it offers the best view of Manhattan!'

So, was it quiet there? The first time that I visited the park, it was—for it was a weekday. However, when I returned with friends on a weekend, it was a different story. The place was enlivened with lots of families, picnics and laughter. And, suspending my quest for quietude, I went along with the flow. *That* was the magic of Long Island! Everyone in our group urged me to surprise them with some tricks up my sleeve.

Switch without a Hitch

With the help of a magic rub, one card changes into another

MATERIAL REQUIRED:
A deck of playing cards.

PREPARATION: Make sure that the card you wish to use as a replacement is the topmost card in the deck, and the card that you wish to replace is directly under it. Here we are changing the 5 of Hearts into a 5 of Clubs. Place the spectator directly in front of you. They should be looking down at the cards in your hand.

THE TRICK DECODED

① Hold the deck of cards in one hand.

② Cover-flip the topmost card and then cover the deck with the other hand.

    ⓐ To do so, place your little finger under the second card and separate the first two cards from the rest of the deck.

    ⓑ Very neatly, so that the spectator sees only the topmost card, flip the first two cards together. This reveals the face of the second card to the spectator. Your Cover-flip is complete!

③ When you place your hand on top of the deck, gently push the topmost card upwards a little. This will expose a bit of the second card.

④ Now use the fleshy part of your palm at the base of your thumb—the thenar—to pull back the second card until it slips free from the pack.

⑤ Push forward and this card should slide over the pack to become the new topmost card. This move will be hidden from view from your spectator who should be viewing the move from above, looking down at the back of your hand.

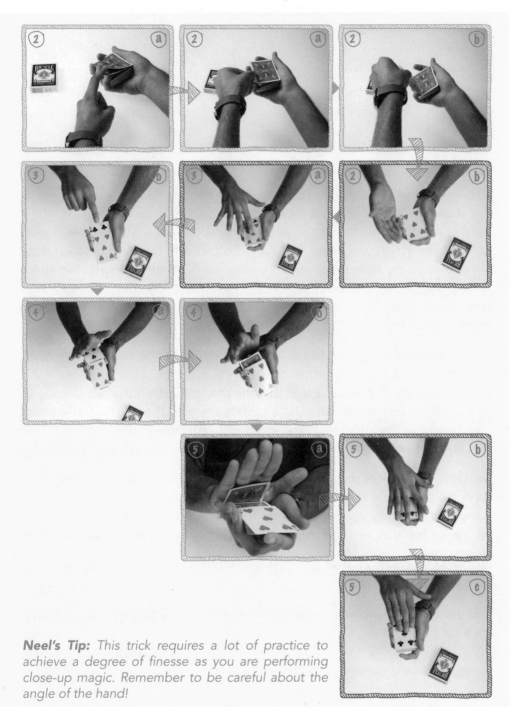

Neel's Tip: This trick requires a lot of practice to achieve a degree of finesse as you are performing close-up magic. Remember to be careful about the angle of the hand!

Close-up magic involves tricks that can be performed for a small group of people who are sitting very close to the magician. This requires very clean and swift moves by the magician as the spectators can see every move. The most popular items used for this branch of magic are commonly available household objects, such as coins, cards and handkerchiefs.

Back in Boston, I was walking down a rather broad street, heading towards the subway—the T. I had just spent a day at the Museum of Fine Arts which houses an incredible collection of paintings by Claude Monet, the French painter. The street was clean, wide and dotted with tall trees on each side. I was lost in my own musings, throwing cards in the air, catching them before they fell to the ground, drawing patterns in my curious head about what else I could do with them to make the bits of ordinary coloured paper more interesting!

And then something caught my eye. I noticed that the streets were filled with yellow maple leaves strewn all over, and in abundance. These were the dried remnants of autumn, a sign that the season had left the wondrous city of Boston. Scattered among the yellow were also those green ones that had been plucked untimely. The wind did not differentiate between the two and swept each colour on the canvas of the road with equal fervour.

And boy, sometimes the green looked yellow and the yellow looked green! As if the same leaf flipped over and changed colour. This was absolutely surreal. It was nature's way of saying that all mute life forms around us are alive in some manner, constantly adding colour and meaning to the world.

Not only that, nature had also just given me a new way to play with my cards. I was ecstatic!

You see, this is how some quiet time and introspection can do wonders for you!

Swap with a Snap

A regular playing card changes into another with a snap of the fingers

MATERIAL REQUIRED:
A deck of playing cards.

PREPARATION: Take two cards—both facing down—and hold them together. These two cards must be shown to the spectator as one card.

THE TRICK DECODED

① Hold the cards together lengthwise by placing your index and middle fingers along their bottom edge. Place your thumb behind these fingers on the other plane of the cards, at the corner of the hidden card. The spectator should see the first card. Let's call it card 1—here, the 6 of Hearts. To maintain authenticity, you can also show the back plane of the card to the spectator—which is actually the back of card 2. Here, card 2 is the King of Spades.

② Release the grip of the index finger and use your middle finger to slide card 1 backwards. At the same time, push the card originally at the back—which is card 2—forward with your thumb. This motion is similar to snapping with your middle finger and thumb. As you pull back card 2 with your ring finger, make sure to push your thumb slightly forward. This will help card 1 snap back into place!

③ Card 1 will be hidden from the audience's view by the angle that you perform the sleight at. It is perpendicular to the plane of card 2. Make sure to flick the top corner of card 1 at the same time that you make the snapping motion. The flicking noise will muffle the sound of the card snapping back.

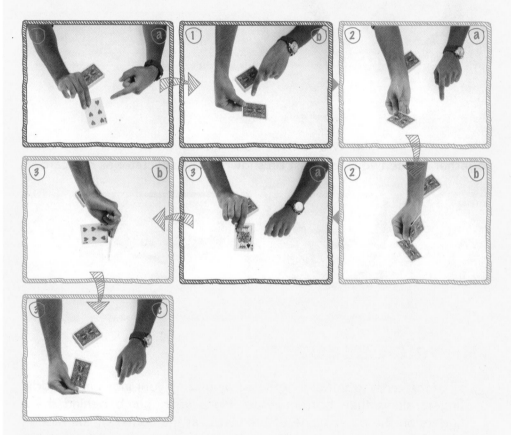

Neel's Tip: *This is an angle-bound trick, so make sure that the spectator is standing directly in front of you.*

Boston's famed Museum of Fine Arts has a mesmerizing collection of paintings by the Impressionist painter Claude Monet. His artistic growth across his career is easily discernible—from the plein-air landscape paintings that he did in the 1860s to the nature paintings, underlining the play of light on different subjects, in the 1880s.

After three eventful months, my trip came to a close. It seemed to be over all too soon but still, I was happy to go home. But back in Mumbai, I had no answer to that one question that everyone seemed to be curious about.

'Bro, what was the best moment that made your trip memorable?'

How does one explain that there were *so many* momentous—magical—occasions? Was it my trip to Florida, where I became a child at Disney World? That enchanted land where children, teenagers and adults alike get lost? The interplay of music and magic there was fascinating—it was almost as if magic was following me.

Or wait—was it my brief rendezvous with a master of the art? It was!

One Friday, while in Boston, I had gone to attend the 'family weekend' at Harvard Business School. There, I'd met a professor, Stephen Thomke, who'd delivered a talk on out-of-the-box thinking for senior executives to implement in extremely competitive environments—about how one can use magic techniques in business to bring about innovative change in productivity. How interesting, right? Mr Thomke had been extremely energetic and motivational. And guess what—he had also invited the world-famous magician-cum-mentalist Jason Randal as part of the demonstration! Being able to see the legend in person was a dream come true for a young magician like me.

The class was thus not a mere lecture but a brilliant orchestration—a dollar bill ripped into small bits, then reappearing as a whole bill inside an orange; spoons energized to bend; wristwatches disappearing! After the class, Mr Thomke had arranged for me to personally interact with Randal for half an hour. And so there I had been, standing face-to-face with one of the world's best close-up magicians!

Obviously I had been awestruck and requested him to show me even more tricks. Everything from mentalism to real illusion! And he'd ended up showing me pure magic for a good two hours, one to one, with the session going on till quite late into the night. But the magician hadn't stopped!

In wonder I had watched his fine fingers move with extreme precision—he'd had me mesmerized with his skill. And there I'd stood, stupefied, at this man's dexterity. He was not only a magician but also a musician—he had scored music for TV and Hollywood. He'd played the piano for me and, not able to resist the temptation, I'd played some notes for him as well. The half-an-hour-long meeting had, by then, extended to three hours. Then, he'd showed me more tricks, and some more . . .

But there was one illusion that Mr Randal had floored me with.

Pit the Orange

The magician takes a card and tears it up. Then, taking one small piece of the torn card, they magically procure the restored card from inside an orange

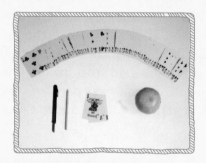

MATERIAL REQUIRED:
Two identical playing cards, an orange, a full deck of playing cards, a knife, a pencil and superglue.

PREPARATION:

① Take one of the two identical cards. Tear a piece from the upper left corner of the card and keep the piece aside. You can tuck it away in your pocket or any other place where you can quickly retrieve it from while performing the trick. Ensure that it is hidden from the spectator's view!

② Take an orange and, using a knife, carefully make a small cut on the top, at the bumpy tip where the stalk was once attached. Keep aside the severed segment. Insert the pen inside the orange and move it around a bit to create a hollow space for the card to go in.

③ Take the card which had its corner torn off and roll it tightly. Now carefully insert the rolled-up card inside the orange, and then seal the orange by attaching the segment using superglue.

Be extremely careful while preparing this because the orange should not look like it has been tampered with. Your gimmick is ready!

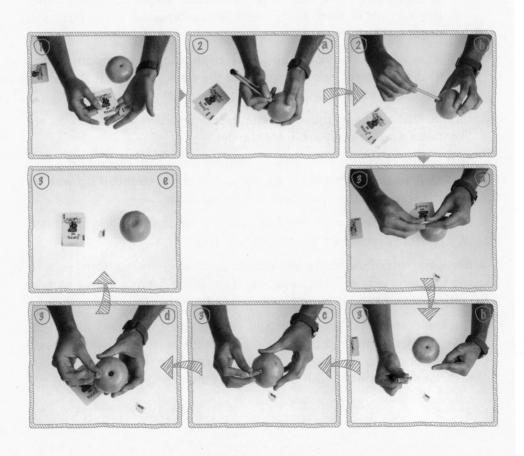

THE TRICK DECODED

① Place the spectator directly in front of you. Begin by shuffling the deck of cards in a seemingly random fashion. However, in your mind, remember the identical card that needs to be picked for the trick. Shuffle the deck face down in such a way that your chosen card stays right at the bottom. Mark this card with the help of the Thumb Break.

  ⓐ Hold the deck face down. Use your thumb to cut the deck into two from anywhere in the middle.

  ⓑ As you do so, the index and middle fingers of your right hand will firmly grip the selected card at the bottom.

  ⓒ With the index and middle fingers of your left hand at the top edge, and your left thumb at the bottom edge of the deck, hold the last card in place as you cut a few sections out of the deck and proceed to shuffle.

  ⓓ After a few rounds of shuffling, which should seem randomly done to the spectator, show the base of the deck to them. It shows the selected card.

② Pick up that card and show it to the spectator again. Make sure to act like it was a completely arbitrary choice!

③ Tear up the card into small pieces. Bring out the torn piece of the first card that you had kept aside earlier and pretend to mix it up with all the small pieces of the completely torn-up card.

④ Now take the piece from the first card and present it to the spectator as a random piece from the pile of torn bits.

⑤ Move the rest of the torn pieces aside, displaying the one torn piece to the spectator again. Then randomly pick up the orange from a natural setting, such as the refrigerator or a fruit basket.

⑥ Cut the orange and show your audience the restored card which you have magically produced from inside a random fruit. They'll be even more shocked to see that the arbitrary torn piece that you picked out fits together perfectly with the card from the orange!

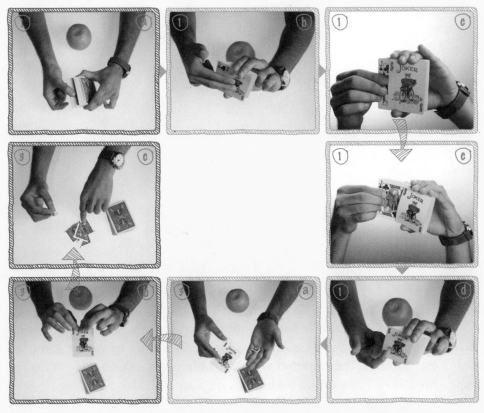

Neel's Tip: *In the concluding step, cut the orange from the middle and stop as soon as your knife strikes the surface of the card. Pull and open the two halves of the orange, revealing the card. Ensure that you never put the knife on top of the orange which has been glued back. This may cause the severed and stuck segment to fall off!*

Jason Randal, the Mad Mentalist, is far more than just a magician and popular figure. Apart from over a hundred television appearances and performing for over twelve heads of states, Randal is a singer, songwriter and knows how to play five different instruments. He has a PhD in psychology and also holds a seventh-degree black belt in karate. A movie and TV actor, he is also a board certified hypnotherapist, a professional scuba instructor, a flight instructor and a special-effects pyrotechnics operator. That's a lot for one man to be, right? Well, that's what magic is!

Stars in the Sky

After returning from the United States, I decided that I was going to pursue my undergraduate studies back home, in Mumbai. I had been in two minds, confused between India and the US, but a long conversation with Mr Ashok Advani, chairman of *Business India* and a family friend, helped me set my sights on Mumbai. The meeting with Mr Advani left a deep imprint on my mind; he advised me on how one can be successful and compassionate at the same time. I was fascinated that such an accomplished man was so down to earth and accessible. He convinced me to choose Mumbai because of its work ethos—and so my decision was made.

I was going to live with my parents in Mumbai, and, along with my studies, continue my magical pursuits. To guide me through the next few months, I had a book gifted by Mr Jason Randal.

Starting my Bachelor of Commerce course at the H.R. College of Commerce and Economics brought with it the promise of a new dawn. Everything that lay ahead of me wore the shining armour of freshness. This was the time for innovation, for challenging myself. And I was as ready as I could be for whatever would come my way!

Mumbai, the city of dreams, has reveries woven every day into its cloudy skies. Some survive and sparkle. Some wander behind the clouds and hang in the vacuum above its metropolitan skyline. And one evening, as I gazed up at the night sky—which glimmered not so much because of the stars but because of the twinkling lights of the high-rise buildings—I decided that I wanted to paint Mumbai's azure sky red with streaks of magic.

College was a very busy affair. At all times, one or the other activity kept me engaged, even beyond class hours and sometimes till late into the evening. After the long day, I would usually board the train from the crowded Churchgate station to Bandra, from where I would often take an autorickshaw back to my house on Carter Road. One particular evening, as I was following the same routine, an event transpired that changed my entire perspective on magic in the most enriching manner. It also marked a moment of real inspiration in my journey as a magician.

As we tootled along the long arc of Carter Road, the autorickshaw driver started lamenting about the congestion in the city, the late hours that he had to work and about Mumbai at large. Like many in this city, he had migrated here from a small town in search of a livelihood. As we talked, I discovered—much to my surprise—that the driver—whom I was calling Bhaiya by now—had a bachelor's degree from Gorakhpur University! He was educated, aware and a conscious citizen—but was driving an autorickshaw. He sighed and told me that a lot of people from his state who come to Mumbai for a better life are educated, but have been compelled to take up blue-collar jobs because of the lack of better opportunities. Bhaiya was one such man—and he had an opinion on many things, from politics to world affairs.

On hearing his story, I wondered for a long time about how I could brighten up his evening, especially since I didn't really have anything that would interest him. That's when I decided to attempt something with whatever objects were there in my pocket—my tiny collection of coins and rubber bands.

For the next hour, my spectator and I sat on a ledge on the Bandra seaside promenade in front of my house. And one after the other, I kept producing random things from my pocket and entertaining him with tricks. Watching my hand, the man's expression changed several times—from confused to surprised to very happy. He couldn't believe his eyes! He said he'd never seen anything like it before and continued to marvel at the tricks. His eyes shone with amazement and his face wore a huge smile. It seemed that the burden of an entire day's work had been taken off his shoulders. That moment I realized that magic could bring unprecedented joy to ordinary people's lives—and isn't that tantamount to moving mountains?

That evening, I reached a turning point. The simple line, 'Chalo, Bhaiya, let me show you some magic!' to the exhausted auto driver, changed the perspective with which I viewed my hobby.

I was starting to learn that a routine should begin with something simple, warming the person up for more advanced tricks. It is not the difficulty of the trick that matters, it is just that the presentation should connect with the person you are performing for.

And one particular trick made Bhaiya totally ecstatic because, by the end of it, he had magically gained some extra bucks.

Chameleon Currency

A banknote of one currency changes into another

MATERIAL REQUIRED:
One ten-rupee banknote, one dollar bill, glue stick.

PREPARATION:

① Take the ten-rupee note and fold it thrice—first, down the middle, widthwise; then, down the middle along the longer edge; lastly, down the middle along the shorter edge.

② Apply glue on half of the back plane of the folded note.

③ Stick the top edge of the folded note on the lower edge of the reverse of the dollar bill. Your gimmick is ready!

THE TRICK DECODED

① Place the spectator directly in front of you and show the dollar bill to them, holding it straight, at the corner, so that the face of the bill is visible to the spectator.

② Fold the dollar bill thrice—just like you folded the ten-rupee note—in front of the spectator, so that the ten-rupee note remains perfectly concealed. To ensure this, maintain the folds strictly according to the ten-rupee note that you're holding behind the dollar bill with your thumb.

③ Find the fold that goes down the middle of the ten-rupee note and unfold it. Remember—its folds are exactly the same as those on the dollar bill, so when you open it, it will look like you are slowly 'changing' the dollar bill. Pull the ten-rupee note open. The spectator will see that the dollar bill has changed to a ten-rupee note!

④ Now the bill is stuck to the reverse of the ten-rupee note—the spectator cannot see it. Clip it with your index and middle finger.

⑤ Pull the bill back with your right hand so that it gets detached from the ten-rupee note. Clip it on both sides of your middle finger and conceal it by loosely closing your palm. While you do this, ensure that the face of the note is in front of the spectator as you did with the dollar bill in step 1. Now you can give the ten-rupee note to the spectator for them to inspect it.

Neel's Tip: *You'll have to be very neat and careful with your folding and pasting skills to pull off this trick successfully.*

While my time at Doon was indeed extraordinary, the years I spent in Mumbai were equally significant. So if I were given the option of going back in time to relive any one phase of my life, I guess both would emerge as uncrowned winners. While the Doon School ignited in me the thirst to learn outside the classroom, Mumbai moulded my dreams as craftily as a sand-smith would make tall castles out of rudimentary, coarse beach sand.

My home doubled up as my magician's workshop, where all sorts of 'sorcery' took place. I lived in one of the most picturesque and breezy areas of the city. The windows of our house opened out to the sea, the sea breeze wafting in—which carried various other smells, especially that of fish. My mother was my 'Guinea Pig Number One'—I tried all my tricks on her first—and my ivory-painted apartment by the sea, my studio. During the holidays, I also visited our house in Delhi, where I had a larger audience—my brother, my grandmother and my chacha. And when *they* were bored, our support staff became the guinea pigs!

You see, I was finally engrossed and neck-deep in magic.

In Mumbai, I had become *Jaaduwala Bhaiya* for the children in our residential block. To entertain the kids, I started with performing tricks using coins as they are available with anyone across all age groups. Lightweight, easy to carry around and a thing of utility, coins are also one of the most important objects in one's everyday toolkit, magician or otherwise. I really loved surprising kids with my tricks because, naive as most of them are, they were my harshest critics. Showing them magic was akin to inviting a challenge upon myself, by which I could constantly better my act. This was also the time in my life when the possibility of being a professional magician or illusionist dawned on me. Till now, the thought of magic as a fully fledged career had not taken shape in my mind. It had only been a pastime, a hobby, a passion. But not any more. I was now Jaaduwala Bhaiya!

Tap and Poof!

K♣

A coin placed on the palm is tapped with a pencil. The pencil vanishes first, only to reappear and make the coin vanish

♣K

> **MATERIAL REQUIRED:**
> A coin, which is not too thick, and a pencil.

PREPARATION: Place the spectator directly in front of you. Ensure that there is enough distance between you and the spectator so that the pencil remains concealed from the spectator when you make it 'vanish'.

THE TRICK DECODED

① Place the coin on the palm of your left hand, at the base of your fingers. Take a pencil in your right hand.

② Holding the pencil at the tip, strike the coin hard two or three times to distract the spectator. The motion of the consecutive taps should be done in such a way that the hand comes down from as high as your head. This will adapt the audience to this movement and they will not doubt your final step. The whole time, you need to be facing perpendicular to your spectator's line of vision. This way, they cannot see the length of the pencil when you tuck it behind your ear in the next step.

③ Now, on the final tap, raise the pencil up to the side of your head as before and tuck it, in a swift move and without missing a beat, behind your ear.

④ Immediately, direct the spectator's attention to the still-visible coin by clipping it between the thumb and index finger of your left hand. As they wonder about the vanished pencil, turn your head to the side and point at the pencil lodged behind your right ear, revealing part of the trick to the spectator. Employ misdirection and put the coin in your pocket as you turn your head.

⑤ As you turn back to face the spectator, keep your left hand closed in a fist. The spectator will think that you still have the coin in your hand. Strike your closed fist with the pencil twice or thrice.

⑥ Open your fist with a sharp tap to reveal your empty palm—the coin has vanished.

Misdirection is a technique of deception employed by magicians to distract the spectator from paying close attention to a secret move that is vital for the trick's execution. Misdirection can be employed by revealing a small part of the trick to misdirect the spectator from another move. In the above illusion, the magician reveals the trick of the pencil vanishing to distract the audience's attention from the coin being put in the pocket.

My collegiate studies were supplemented by numerous opportunities that Mumbai allows students to explore. And this was an incredible experience for me. In fact, beyond the realm of academics, there were the worlds of theatre, dance, sport, music and more. My friends and I would often sit for hours in the canteen, discussing all kinds of things while we indulged in Chinese food and nimbu pani. However, while in college, I didn't let most of the other students even get a whiff of my inclination towards magic as a hobby. Till, as part of an advertising and marketing course, my classmates and I were asked to create a campaign. The project was more like a super-class, under the guidance of my rather curious teacher, Mrs Rajeshwari. She was stringent about timing, timing and timing! If we were even a minute late, she'd—would you believe it—make us stand on the bench; if we were ten minutes late, we had to do an extra internship; and if we missed a class, we were dismissed from her course. But we respected her because she trained us well.

The advertising project that we had to create would eventually be evaluated by a group of senior professionals from the industry as well as our college teachers. The task given to us was to come up with a campaign for an energy drink. Interestingly, the tag line of this popular energy drink said it 'gives you wings'. And I thought to myself—*why not take the exact tag line forward?*

So, after the presentation on the campaign, I decided to give an added dimension to the tag line. In front of a full house in the auditorium, I solemnly walked up to the edge of the stage, faced the audience and said, 'If you don't believe that the drink gives you wings, I will prove it!'

I placed a can of the drink on the floor of the stage and concentrated on it. Then I waved my hands and, magically, the can levitated upwards, towards me—and I caught it in style.

The audience, comprising advertising experts, college teachers and students, was spellbound. My team and I got a rapturous ovation. This demanding trick (one should start with the relatively easier illusion of levitating a card) brought me instant popularity, giving wings to my dreams. We won the award for putting up the best presentation too!

Card in the Air

A random card is selected from a deck of playing cards in front of the spectator. The card is placed flat on the magician's palm which, after a subtle wave of their other hand, levitates in the air

MATERIAL REQUIRED:
A deck of playing cards, glue or Sellotape, scissors or a paper cutter, and a clear strip of flexible plastic (which can easily be found in the packaging of a new shirt).

PREPARATION: **Place the spectator directly in front of you.**

① Cut the plastic strip to the width of approximately 1.5 cm. Make sure that the strip is slightly longer than the length of the card.

② Bend the strip at a 90-degree angle two-thirds of the way along its length, so that the bent plane marks the edge of the card when you paste the strip on it.

③ Stick the strip on the back of the card, at the midpoint of the edge. Make sure that you stick the centre of the strip to the centre of the back of the card. Only use a spot of glue or a small piece of clear tape—do not put glue on the entire card. Let it dry. 1 mm of the length of the plastic strip should stick out from the card.

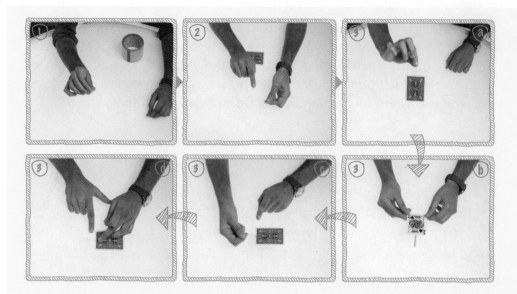

THE TRICK DECODED

1. Place the card on your left hand, facing upwards. Keep the card diagonally across the palm, so that the end with the strip touches the side of your palm.

2. Once you've shown the spectator that the card is resting on your palm, pin the bent end of the strip on the side of the wrist, gently, with your right hand. This will increase the pressure on one side of the card, causing the other side to rise in the air.

3. To conceal the view of your right hand pinning the strip, release and extend all your fingers, letting only your thumb press the strip. The other fingers can loosely hover above the 'floating' card, to give the impression that the force from your right hand is making the card float in the air!

Neel's Tip: *Practise this trick in front of a mirror to figure out the exact angle at which your spectator should be placed so that the plastic strip is concealed.*

Magic had, by now, suddenly become synonymous with my identity. I was Neel 'Magic' Madhav. Ever-ready for a performance, I even started carrying around a pack of cards in my pocket.

But *why* did I do magic?

Because magic has the power to make people happy. In today's world, when everyone seems stressed about something or the other, if I am able to make a difference, however small, isn't that worth pursuing? Magic for me is about creating an experience that the viewer will remember for the rest of their life.

One such occasion had been my encounter with the auto-driver Bhaiya. And another was shortly after I had met the magician James Randi in Goa. I'd had a conversation with him for almost four hours, and the meeting had been priceless. I'd felt like the luckiest person to have had the opportunity to spend so much time with him, a legend who has reams of literature written about his skills.

I was back at the hotel, in the business centre, seated next to a man; and we started chatting. He had come to Panjim from his village for some work. As he seemed rather tense and I sensed it, I asked him what was wrong. Then he told me his life story. He explained that, for some time, he had been struggling and could barely make ends meet. And that he was even more nervous at the time because his business was suffering. After getting a little teary-eyed, he asked me what I did for a living. Immediately, I told him that I did magic, at which he inquired if I did *real* magic.

And as I performed for him, trick by trick, his expression changed. From a grin to a smile to a burst of laughter. It almost felt like he'd forgotten all his worries in a moment of amazement—and I couldn't believe that I'd encouraged him to feel that way.

Card Magnet

A ♠
A ♠

An entire deck of cards is flung towards the ceiling; the signed card is found stuck on the ceiling while the rest fall off

MATERIAL REQUIRED:
A deck of playing cards, a pen, one size 19 rubber band, and magician's wax or Sellotape.

PREPARATION: Take the magician's wax or Sellotape and put it on your thumbnail if you are performing this trick at a distance from the spectator. If not, put it on the underside of your finger or under the table or any place where you can retrieve it from without it being apparent to the spectator.

THE TRICK DECODED

① Make the spectator choose a card and ask them to sign it.

② Put the signed card back in the deck and place it on the top slyly by marking the position of the signed card using the Thumb Break.

③ Take the rubber band and wrap it around the deck diagonally. Start from the top. The card has four corners where 1 and 2 are parallel, 2 and 3 are perpendicular, and 3 and 4 are parallel. Loop the rubber band around corners 2 and 4.

④ While you're wrapping the rubber band around corner 4, deploy the Pinkie Break, in which the top card is elevated above the loop. Be sure to wrap the band under the signed card which is on top, and around corner 2. The wrapping process is complete.

⑤ Now, to make the topmost card stick to the ceiling when you throw the deck upwards, you have to use magician's wax. Retrieve the concealed wax or tape and, using your index finger, spread it on the centre of the signed card. This move is a second's work, as you only need to slap it on to the back of the card. A gesture of gripping the card can also conceal this move from the spectator.

⑥ Take the entire deck and throw it up towards the ceiling. This has to be done with a smooth, swirling motion of the wrist. The signed card should go spinning up with the right amount of force. Do remember that the force with which you fling the card has to be sufficient for it to stick.

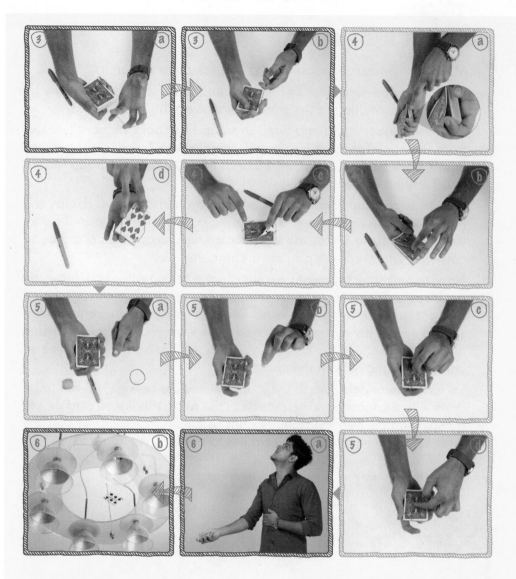

Neel's Tip: This trick can involve as many spectators as you like. This is a perfect gimmick for big parties where many people are present and each one will have a souvenir—their individual signed cards—to take back home. Ensure that the ceiling is smooth, and not grainy or rough, so that the card can stick easily.

The Pinkie Break is a very important move when it comes to card magic. By mastering the Pinkie Break, one can mark any position in a deck of cards, giving the magician control over the trick. The move can be used in various card tricks.

If you want to amaze your audience with an illusion using this method, ask them to pick out a random card from the deck. After seeing the card, ask them to place this card anywhere in the middle of the deck. By using the Pinkie Break, mark the position where your spectator has inserted the card. When you pull out the same card that they'd randomly inserted, your spectator will be amazed. If you master this, a lot of your card tricks are taken care of. Just follow these simple steps:

1. Take a deck of playing cards and hold it in your left palm. Cup the edge of the deck with your fingers. Your thumb will be placed on the top left of the deck.

2. Now ask the spectator to pick any card, see it and put it back in the deck at any random position.

3. Keep the grip of your fingers loose as the spectator puts back the card.

4. Press your little finger above the card that the spectator has just inserted. This will mark the position of the card.

5. Press your thumb on the edge, on top of the deck. This will ensure that the plane of the card is even and will hide the Pinkie Break.

6. Retrieve your card from the marked position whenever your trick requires it.

During my summer break, I interned at one of India's top radio stations, Red FM, and then followed it with another internship at a production house called Sphere Origins. I was referred to Sunjoy Waddhwa and Comall Waddhwa of the company through a friend of the family and, very soon, the duo took me under their wing. Sphere Origins is one of the largest television production houses in the country and, upon joining, I could see why. I was assigned to a new show and would spent long hours with the dedicated team to get the production under way. During this stint, I learnt how to dabble in creativity and assist large-scale productions. Eventually, I also learnt that delivering on time is important and can be a tough task. It was a significant lesson that would stand me in good stead when I would do my own TV programme. In fact, Sunjoy and Comall follow my journey and progress even today.

During my internship I noticed that the late nights would get very stressful for the entire production unit. So I did what I knew best. I helped elevate the mood through my illusions. In Mumbai, no one believed my chosen career option. People in the city expected and accepted more glamorous avenues—a fashionably dressed actor, a budding director, a cool sound engineer, a focused cinematographer, a balmy musician. But a *jaadugar*? *That* seemed rather far-fetched! Most had, at the time, seen well-known, international close-up magicians on television but an Indian illusionist was still new on the horizon. So some even smirked at me, asking, 'Do you release pigeons out of a box?'

The first time I saw magic being performed, I was probably around five. My parents had called a party magician for a birthday, and he'd come dressed in his bright sherwani, complete with a magician's hat. In a very loud voice, he'd said, '*Gilly gilly choo!*'

Soon the show got under way. As soon as he started doing something with his wand or his hands, every kid focused on him intently. Everyone stopped talking and all started paying close attention. As if the very motive of every kid's life was to catch out the magician! Each kid wanted to figure out the trick before the other, because everyone wanted to prove themselves smarter than the rest. And just when the magician completed his move— as if in the Olympic 100-metre race—each one wanted the quickest start. All the kids sprang up and start pointing at the magician, saying, 'You did this trick like that!' Even though no one had a clue how it was done, they still shouted and screamed, trying to figure out the mystery behind the magic.

Do you know why that happened? I'm sure you've done it too.

This is the constraint of the magician. The art of performing magic isn't just about doing some random card trick to entertain a bunch of people but also about taking them on a journey in which the wow factor sets in.

So what is the process of magic?

The process is not just about the tricks and gimmicks, it's also about handling various situations and audiences, come what may. Magic, when performed, is also about learning communication skills, especially when facing a large group of people. It's the same process that every single person follows to reach their own individual goals. Although it is the same for most, the way the process unfolds is different for each one of us.

It was different for me too. Back when I was in school, I wasn't the brightest student because, for some reason, rote academics just did not sit well with me. I used to look at the others and ask myself why it was so tough for me to study and not for them. So, during this phase of my life, I tried to find a process for myself that would help me study. A process that would keep me from getting distracted.

And I did find my process, especially in magic. The more I read about it, the more I knew about it. The more knowledge I accumulated, the more easily I could use those techniques. These very techniques helped me strengthen my process. And I stuck to my lesson; everything changed. I could focus better, I would get distracted less often. I could figure out ways to do things that I couldn't have even come up with back in my schooldays. Now I can even understand chemistry and physics! And, along with magic, I continued with music—I regularly practised playing the sitar, the piano and the guitar; I even composed some music. This helped me to keep my mind calm and clutter-free, and be more creative.

Ripped and Restored

A newspaper sheet is ripped into four pieces. The spectator puts a finger on the pieces and they seem to magically restore themselves into a whole newspaper sheet

MATERIAL REQUIRED:
Two identical newspapers.

PREPARATION: Before beginning the trick, crumple one newspaper sheet without tearing it. Conceal it in the underside of your palm before you start your performance. Your gimmick is ready! Ensure that the spectator is directly in front of you at all times.

THE TRICK DECODED

1. Start the trick with the whole newspaper sheet in front of you and fold it into quarters, creasing the paper, and then unfold it. Explain to your spectator that doing this makes it easier to tear the paper evenly.

2. Hold the sheet in front of you, facing the audience—the other torn and crushed paper should be pressed by your thumb against the whole

sheet. Rip the whole newspaper sheet down the middle and tear it into four pieces. Keep the crushed paper concealed throughout.

3) Now crush the paper that you just tore. Keep it towards the front of your palm, so that the other crushed paper is hidden behind it. While using both your hands to squeeze the newly crushed paper into a ball, swiftly shift the torn piece to your right hand.

4) Keeping the torn paper concealed, stretch out your left hand to give the 'restored' piece to the spectator.

5) Misdirect—the spectator will be distracted when you present the crushed paper to them—and place the balled-up torn newspaper in your pocket.

6) Ask the spectator to examine the newspaper that you have handed them. They will find that it is in one piece!

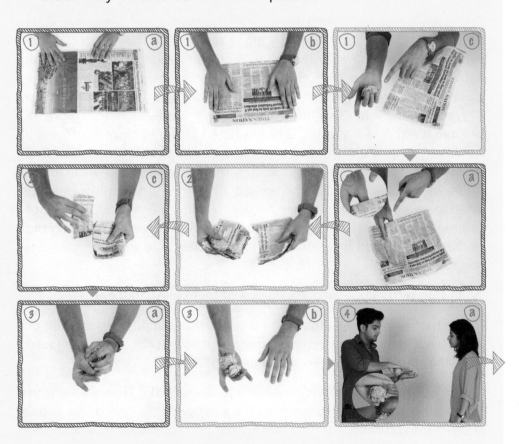

Mumbai, where dreams are made but also broken. A city in which each one—with stars in their eyes—is trying to carve a small—or mammoth—niche for themselves.

I was too.

One evening, as I was walking back home from Bandstand, two young boys stopped me short. And how did they do that? They started reciting movie dialogues one after the other. All those famous lines—by Amitabh Bachchan, Shah Rukh Khan, Salman Khan, you name it. Bandstand, where most of the bigwigs of the film industry reside, was just a few turns from where I lived. It opens right on to the ocean and the Bandra Fort isn't far from it either. As a result, it has bubbled into a hotspot for Mumbai's crowds—young men, women, kids, and the hawkers serving hot street food. People are always about in Bandstand, taking long walks or just sitting by the sea watching the sunset. And right in the middle of it all, the duo even broke into dance moves, leaving me thoroughly amused and entertained. When they asked for money—the fee for enjoying their performance—I told them that I was a magician. And instantly, their eyes brightened up.

'Bhaiya, show us some jaadu!' said one of them in excitement.

I had a marker with me with which I drew a variety of patterns on their tiny hands while they entertained me with their stories. Longingly, they looked up at the stars and said, 'We also want to be stars one day!'

And so our little party of tricks went on for some time. Then we went to a coffee shop around the corner, and the boys were delighted with a treat of brownies and cake. Thankful and happy, they continued their antics and I, mine, before we finally parted ways into the night.

Money Express-o

Some coffee in a cup changes to coins

MATERIAL REQUIRED:
A few coins, two large—and identical—opaque paper cups (named here A and B), some coffee in a third opaque cup, one knife and a piece of sponge cut in the shape of the bottom of the cup.

PREPARATION:

1. Take paper cup A and cut off the top portion—about one-third of the cup.
2. Take the other cup (B) and cut a slit right at the base. This slit should be small enough to be covered by your finger.
3. Now place the sponge—that is shaped exactly like the bottom of the cup—inside cup B. Push it down to the base of the cup.
4. After that, simply put cup A inside cup B but do not push it all the way down. When you begin the trick, the spectator should only be able to see one cup i.e., cup B.
5. Fill cup A with coins.
6. Pour some black coffee on top so that the coins are just under the surface of the liquid. The spectator should only be able to see the coffee in the cup.

Your gimmick is ready!

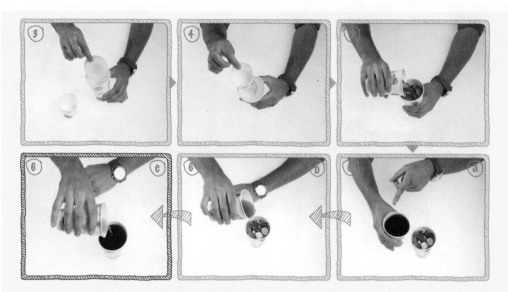

THE TRICK DECODED

1. Go to the spectator with your trick set up, and show them the cup with coffee in it. You can also sip the coffee to make it look authentic.

2. Place your finger at the bottom of cup B, closing the slit and pushing up the sponge that is inside. This will push up cup A, making the coins naturally rise above the surface of the coffee. Your audience will be so amazed that they will only be paying attention to the contents of the cup, and won't notice that it is shrinking in size as the coins appear.

Neel's Tip: *If you are going to drink the coffee in the cup, make sure to wash the coins thoroughly before using them for the trick. And make sure to practise beforehand, so that no liquid spills from the cup, giving the trick away.*

Innovation and You Got Magic

What do you do when you are born with a camera in your hand? You imagine that the camera is a companion who helps you keep forever every image that you see with your eyes.

Let me take you back in time, to when I found a friend in a camera. I filmed with my first camera at the age of nine and learnt to edit a short film at the age of eleven—even before I went to boarding school. My mother is a television professional, and so I grew up accompanying her on her shoots to Gujarat and Rajasthan for a heritage-and-travel show. At a young age, I was asked to use the tripod, position the small video camera and shoot—just like the cameraman. Of course, I was only handed the camera to keep me busy and out of trouble. But the experience still made my young self feel very important, as if I were really part of the crew. But when I was sent to the Doon School, I could not take my two best friends along—my video camera and my tripod.

When I turned eighteen, I was gifted my first Canon, which opened up a new world of colour and light for me. A world that I could capture with a click! And click I did—as much as I could. My camera travelled with me everywhere, slung around my shoulder. As my colleague would go on to say later, 'It's literally got its arm around your shoulders, Neel!'

My journey through the lens soon merged paths with my magical voyage.

During one of my internships, we travelled to Rajasthan looking for locations. And my first brush with work-related photography brought me to the perfect location—Udaipur. I travelled there as part of a television crew, the production team in particular. We had to shoot all the stunning palaces—the City Palace, the Shiv Niwas Palace, the Fateh Prakash Palace, the Taj Lake Palace. By the end of the location shoot, I could only dream of palaces! However, Rajasthan is more than just palaces and my camera was not content. It wanted to capture more 'wow 'images.

Many consider Udaipur to be India's most magical destination. While there, I sometimes felt that the camera had a mind of its own, for it took some incredible images—rendering the rays of the sun in their sevenfold magnificence, recording the flight of birds against the background of the Fateh Prakash Palace, arresting the ripples in Lake Pichola with the majestic Taj Lake Palace in the background. As if it were capturing the soul of a city in a memory card.

Rajasthan isn't just about its dunes either. There's an element of mysticism attached to the state, beyond its vast stretches of desert. It is a true hidden gem in Rajasthan, rightly called the Venice of the East because of its picturesque beauty, adorned by the shimmering Lake Pichola with a steady trail of the Aravallis surrounding it. Udaipur is the most romantic verse in the passage of India. Fascinating palaces, temples and havelis, and countless crooked, colourful streets make for the perfect setting for anyone with a love for luxury, indulgence and grandeur.

This distinct quality of Udaipur—that sets it apart from the rest of this country—can be felt when one sits by the lake, watching the captivating scene of the sun setting behind the Taj Lake Palace, or when one is taking a walk in the local market right behind Lake Pichola, eyes dazzled by the leather and silk artefacts. Udaipur has it all—from food to nature's bounty—and is truly beautiful! And to entertain my fellow crew-members on our scenic travels, I kept them engaged with many tricks.

A lakeside performance in Udaipur, this next trick can be found on our YouTube channel!

Float the Note

K ♣
♣ K

The magician takes a banknote in their hand and crumples it. Then they take a glass and place it over the crumpled note. When the glass is inverted, the note starts floating inside the glass

> **MATERIAL REQUIRED:**
> A banknote, a transparent glass and two small magnets.

PREPARATION: Take the two magnets and conceal them between the fingers of either hand. Place the spectator directly in front of you.

THE TRICK DECODED

1. Display your palms and show the spectator that there is absolutely nothing in your hands.

2. Pick up a banknote and crumple it into a ball. However, you have to discreetly drop the magnet on the note—the one held between the fingers of the same hand—just before you start crumpling it, to prevent the spectator from seeing the magnet. Once you have crumpled the note completely, show it to the spectator from a distance.

3. Now, as you proceed to pick up the glass, swiftly release the remaining magnet from between your fingers and hold it between your thumb and index finger. Keep it concealed from the spectator and place it on the outer plane of the glass.

4. Invert the glass over the crumpled note in your hand. Bring your thumb—which conceals the second magnet—towards the top of

the glass. This will attract the magnet inside the balled-up note and, instead of remaining at the bottom of the glass, the note will float inside it!

⑤ Remove your hand which was holding the glass once the note has begun floating—this will intensify the effect. The attraction of the magnets will continue to hold the note up.

Neel's Tip: *To heighten the effect, move your thumb slightly and, as you do so, the note will start spinning in the glass!*

And that is how *You Got Magic*, the television show, was conceived. I wanted to capture the magic in each and every beautiful destination of India, not just Rajasthan, for I felt that every town was special and had a soul of its own.

As I understood it, contemporary magic was virtually non-existent on Indian television. It was usually drama, action, comedy and dance that received high ratings. Magic as an art form needed to be appreciated in its modern variety. The first image of a magician that is still the most prevalent is of a guy with a top hat, at a birthday party, surrounded by children. And the most common idea of a 'magical India' is that it is an exotic land of rope tricks, vanishing elephants, dancing snakes and sawing girls in half. So I sincerely believed that magic on Indian television needed to be updated.

The challenge for the programme, however, was to create magic with local items. By now I was convinced that in order to create something special, I needed to go beyond the usual—the cards, rubber bands and coins.

And *how* do you localize magic? My mind started working overtime like my camera, looking for images to snap and local elements to create magic with.

I had learnt about the basics of television production from my mother at her production house and then at Sphere Origins, where I was exposed to larger-than-life productions. And soon the idea of producing a young, innovative and entertaining programme on magic materialized. Several concepts were brainstormed by the vibrant team that came together for this project, and we decided to integrate magic with adventure and travel, making the show contextual and relevant.

Then, at a chance meeting with Mr Prannoy Roy, a doyen in the Indian television and media sector, I had the opportunity to discuss with him what I wanted to do with magic and why I saw television as an appropriate medium to change the image of magic in India. Not only did I discuss the idea behind the show, I also performed a few tricks for him. And he was intrigued! Subsequently he arranged for me to meet with the relevant people in his team. What I found most fascinating about this encounter was that there I was, a mere twenty-year-old, sitting across the table from a legend in the television world—and he was listening to me patiently. Once Mr Roy identified the interesting framework of my idea, he did not hesitate to support me and only had words of encouragement. And as a young lad, those words meant the world to me.

Soon enough, the contours of the programme took shape and it came down to execution. All that I had learnt about planning, strategizing and, above all, creativity would now come to use. And that became the quintessential issue, which all well-known professional magicians are faced with.

How do you create that wow factor which will look magical—episode after episode?

For there is nothing more strenuous than constantly pushing the mind to create new illusions. Professional magicians can't just innovate on a whim; a process must be followed even behind the illusory. And for this, I followed Jason Randal's lessons.

'Magic is strongly linked with the concept of practice and successful magicians are those who have learned the value of that old saying, "practice makes perfect." From an early age, they recognize the need to rehearse regularly. They'll repeatedly perform a sleight-of-hand maneuver for countless hours in front of a mirror until they're satisfied that they've worked out all the kinks. And while they're practicing, they'll also experiment with different ways of doing something in order to find the optimal technique. This process reveals what is visible to an audience from different angles and what will need "hiding" during a performance.'

—Stefan Thomke and Jason Randal on creativity, invention, experimentation and innovation.

'The Magic of Innovation', *European Business Review*, May–June 2014

A full year after the seed was planted, I started shooting for the show, which would go on to become a labour of love. A unique programme, *You Got Magic* combines food, travel and adventure, leaving the audience asking for more. While we treat the audience to some legendary folklore and the stories of the numerous people we meet on our journey, we also perform magic. Real people and real magic!

So we started travelling extensively across the length and breadth of India. It has been one of the most enriching experiences—to meet and interact with so many people from different regions. And I was finally a professional illusionist, out in the world to entertain and amaze. While my television show is rooted in finding the most unique locations in India, there are moments when the landscape of this country and the fabric of its people stupefy me with their own magic. Myriad vividly remembered locales are etched in my mind and I still stand as a spectator gaping at the tricks they played on me.

At the inauguration of an event at Mount Carmel College in Bangalore, my show and I were described quite candidly—

Neel Madhav from *You Got Magic* is not your usual tuxedo-clad, hoarse-toned man who's trying to win your fancy by pulling out a puzzled chicken from his great big black hat. Instead, Neel's charm lies in his youthful, zesty, fun persona mixed with an appalling level of energy, which in turn, rings through the laughs and amazement of his audience. It is rather the childlike wonder in his eyes and the impish grin that together ooze warmth and a sense of familiarity to those around him, which inevitably reflects on the screen in the programme, *You Got Magic*.

Among my first shoots was one in Agra, where I was shooting in Fatehpur Sikri. One afternoon when I had some time off, I visited the Buland Darwaza—the huge gateway to the palace. As I stood marvelling at the sheer beauty of the majestic structure, I spotted a little boy and girl trying to entertain foreigners by talking in a variety of accents. And they could do it all—English, French, Italian, Spanish—you name it. They barely knew the language but they got the accents just right.

I walked up to the duo and, to my surprise, they concocted the most sordid tale but with an impish glint in their eyes. The boy said that what they wanted the most in the world was a decent pair of shoes. This was because the poor siblings would go to school every day wearing simple slippers, and their teacher wouldn't allow them to enter class.

When I said that I only had enough money to buy them one pair of shoes, the brother cracked a joke, saying, 'We'll wear it on alternate days. One day she'll go to school, one day I'll go. And she can put some paper inside a bigger size to wear it, of course!'

I had been trying really hard to keep a straight face but I couldn't help but smile at the two. When I told them I was a magician, they forgot their woeful story and 'Jaadu dikhao!' came the reply in unison.

Genie in a Bottle

A coin larger than the size of the bottleneck penetrates a bottle

K ♣

♣ K

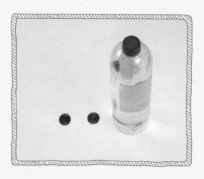

MATERIAL REQUIRED:
Two identical coins (named 1 and 2 here), a half-filled plastic bottle with a brand label, and a knife.

PREPARATION:

1. Make a tiny slit in the neck of the bottle. Ensure that this slit is above the water level and is big enough for the coin to pass through. It is best to make a horizontal cut around the neck of the bottle.

2. Put coin 1 inside the bottle through this slit.

3. Place and keep the spectator directly in front of you at all times.

THE TRICK DECODED

1. Hold the bottle in your hand and show it to the spectator at such an angle that it conceals coin 1—which is inside the bottle—from their view, due to optical illusion. The illusion can be achieved only by placing the spectator exactly in front of you.

2. Ask the spectator for a coin—let this be coin 2. Ensure that it is a coin of the same denomination as coin 1.

3. Hold the bottle still and bring coin 2 towards its lower half.

4. Rub the bottle with your fingers to create an effect of injecting the coin in it. At the same time, shake the bottle to unsettle coin 1 inside.

5. Slide coin 2 down, under the bottle, before you display the bottle to the spectator for examination.

6. Remove the lid of the bottle to reveal that a coin cannot pass through the bottleneck, as it is larger. For this, compare the bottleneck with any coin of the same denomination in front of the spectator.

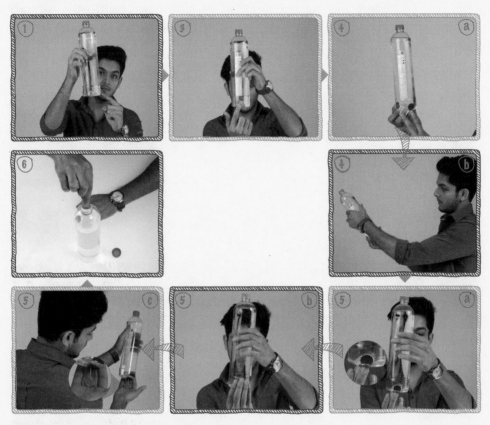

Neel's Tip: *Perform this trick in a dark location or an extremely bright location for a better effect.*

Another shoot took me to the magical land of Jaisalmer. It is popularly called the Golden City because of its rich medieval architecture built purely with yellow sandstone. One of the most striking aspects of Jaisalmer is the Jaisalmer Fort, or the Sonar Quila. Alleys within the fort are populated with stores selling colourful clothes, paintings, metal jewellery and semi-precious stones; hordes of local people and an equal number of curious travellers, mostly foreigners, frequent the bylanes. When one is in such a vibrant place as the Jaisalmer Fort, which is full of eclectic people and eclectic artefacts, one is inspired to pick up just about every article one sees and try doing a trick with it. I was confounded by the numerous alleys around the fort, where each zigzag path opened into a boggling matrix of paths. How could anyone remember their way through the labyrinth? Although I couldn't find my way in those confusing yet carefully designed streets of Jaisalmer, I did find a number of objects that I could weave magic around.

I entered a jewellery shop, whose owner seemed to be a collector of an infinite number of semi-precious stones. He also had a vast collection of coins. Seeing this, and after some conversation, I realized that his store housed the ideal objects for me to perform magic with—which he very kindly allowed me to do.

The Unexpected Bonus

The magician gives the spectator three coins and keeps one in their hand. And, in a flash, the coin in the magician's hand transfers to the spectator's

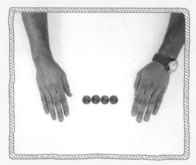

> **MATERIAL REQUIRED:**
> Four identical coins.

PREPARATION: **Place the spectator directly in front of you.**

THE TRICK DECODED

① Start by showing the four coins to the spectator. You can also hand the coins out for them to ensure that they haven't been tampered with.

② Take one coin in your hand and pretend to transfer it to your other hand; close your palm simultaneously to make the spectator believe that the coin is indeed in your other hand now. However, what you need to do is keep the coin concealed in the same hand using the Classic Palm Technique.

③ Now, with the same hand in which the fourth coin is concealed, pick up the other three coins. Give them to your spectator and close their hand to form a fist. When you're doing this, discreetly drop the fourth coin in their hand as well—without them noticing. This step will require a lot of practice.

④ Engage them in conversation and heighten the drama by saying that you will now transfer a coin from your hand to theirs.

⑤ Open your hand to reveal that your coin has vanished. Then tell them to open their fist and leave them in shock as the spectator now has not three, but four coins!

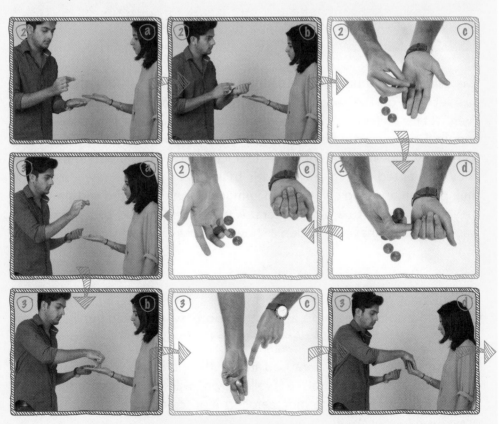

Visit our YouTube channel to watch me stun the shopkeeper!

It is said that one hasn't experienced the true spirit of Rajasthan till one has set foot on the sands of the Sam Sand Dunes. It's lavish, indulgent even. Yet it's a simple pleasure—letting the grains of sand sift between your fingers. On my way to the dunes one afternoon, I met a group of individuals commonly known as *behrupiyas*—artistically inclined wandering minstrels. They enchanted our crew with their tricks and their acts, their song and their performance. So colourful, so immaculate in their attire and show, that they stood out as true entertainers. A while later when I told them that I was a magician, they demanded a show from me too, and I happily obliged.

The team also made a stop at Ranthambore, which, incidentally, was my first time at a national park. And we were there to spot a tiger, of course!

The evening before we ventured inside the park, we met a gentleman over drinks at the hotel, a well-known wildlife photographer. Our team immediately took to him, cajoling him to tell us about some of his previous experiences.

But the gentleman pointedly said, 'I've only come here to spot and shoot one particular tiger!'

'Just *one* particular tiger?' I looked at him in amazement. The gentleman nodded, albeit barely.

'But how can you choose which tiger you will shoot? Isn't it pure luck to even spot a tiger in a national park ?' I persisted.

'She knows when I am around. And usually I do spot her.' He smiled quietly.

No way, I thought to myself, and changed the subject.

The next day, early in the morning, we made our way inside Ranthambore National Park. As we walked ahead, in the depths of Zone 3 of the tiger reserve, the guide explained how approximately fifty tigers had marked their territories throughout the length and breadth of the park, and, in order to save the tiger population, tourists were only allowed entry into a few zones. Eventually we reached a waterbody called Padma Talao, around the Raj Bagh ruins, which is considered a favourite spot for some tigers. That's when I asked our guide about the special tigress that our photographer friend was looking out for.

The guide nodded. 'It is true! There are entire villages around the park that revere this tigress. Her progeny populates most of Ranthambore and she is almost twenty years of age. People worship her as the Queen Mother.'

'Wow! But most tigers die at a much younger age—by fifteen?' Even I had researched a little about tigers as preparation for our trip.

'You are absolutely right, sir! But not this one. She is one hell of a tigress! In fact, she was very fierce once upon a time, protecting her brood with great care!'

'And how do you recognize her?'

'She has a marking on her face, in the shape of a fish. And so she is called Machli.'

Our team was awed by the tales of Machli's feats that the guide narrated to us.

That evening, after an entire day of exploring Ranthambore, we returned to the hotel to share our stories with the others over drinks and dinner. One lady excitedly recounted how she spotted a tiger at a lake from a distance, while I mentioned my sighting of one who was relaxing in a lake—but it was a lazy fellow who'd refused to come out of the cool water. He'd only raised his head to yawn.

The gentleman from the previous evening was there too. He looked up interestedly and I asked him if he had spotted his tigress, Machli.

'Yes, of course! I think she came looking for me,' he answered with a smile. Then, gently, he added, 'I can tell that she has become old—she was walking very slowly. But she still has the warmest eyes. For me, Machli is the mistress of this matrix called Ranthambore National Park.'

In August 2016, however, the Queen of Ranthambore passed away.

Coin Matrix

The magician places four coins on a table and a card on top of each coin. When the magician removes the cards, the coins will have teleported from under one card to another

MATERIAL REQUIRED:
A deck of playing cards, four identical coins and a cloth-covered table.

PREPARATION: Place the four coins on the table, arranged as if each were at the corner of a large box.

THE TRICK DECODED

1. Remove four cards from the deck and place the first card on top of a coin by sliding it off the top of the deck with your thumb. At the same time, secretly pick up the coin and hold it right under the bottommost card with your middle finger. This will hide it from the spectator's view.

2. Now cover the remaining three coins with the other cards with a similar flick of your thumb. Secretly drop the hidden coin as you place the last card over the fourth coin. You should now have four cards in the four corners of the imaginary box—one with no coin under it, one with two coins under it, and two with one coin under it. Be sure to remember which card covers how many coins.

3. Announcing that you will now make the coins teleport, pick up two cards simultaneously—the card with two coins under it and a card with one coin under it. As you pick up the card with one coin under it, secretly pick up the coin as well by pinching it against the bottom of the card.

4. Pull both the cards towards yourself and slide the 'vanished' coin from one card to the other. It's important to do this quickly, as the audience will be distracted by the appearance of the 'new' coin in the two-coin pile.

5. Proceeding quickly, cover the two exposed coins with the card against which you are holding the 'vanished' coin. Slip that coin into the two-coin pile—now there are three coins under this card. Discard the extra card. There should now be three cards laid out—one with three coins under it, another with no coins under it, and a third with one coin under it.

6. Pick up two cards simultaneously—the card with the three coins under it and the card with one coin under it—once again, secretly pinching the single coin against the card as you lift it. It will appear as if you have caused the coin to teleport yet again.

7. Sliding this newly 'vanished' coin over to the card in your other hand, quickly slip the card with the coin now hidden under it on top of the three exposed coins. You now have two cards left—one with no coins under it and one with four coins under it.

8. Slowly lift the card with no coins under it and show that the coin is gone. Lift up the remaining card to reveal all four coins.

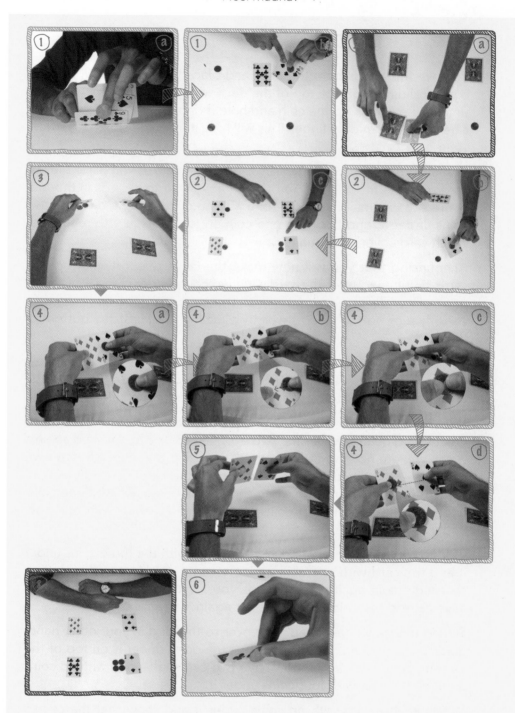

I had never known how fascinating Varanasi is till I travelled there for the show. For three days and two nights, the team basked in the magic of the spiritual capital of India. Located on the banks of the Ganga, Varanasi is considered one of the most pious places for Hindu devotees in India. Fifteen days after Diwali every year, the smell of oil-soaked lamps engulfs the ghats of this abode. When we arrived, the city of Varanasi was gearing up for Dev Deepavali and I was all set to find magic in the divinity.

My team had found the perfect place to stay, from where we could get an unparalleled view of the ghats. The sight was like a film roll, a sequence of different snapshots making up one scene. Sadhus stood in line, dipping into the river; children chanted Vedic mantras; rituals for the dead were being observed in one spot. After shooting for some time within the confines of narrow lanes—which often allowed us to only walk in single file—we somehow managed to reach the ghats in the evening. As the night descended, the steps, aglow with a golden light, were overflowing with the most diverse human population I had ever seen. We had to tread carefully as every inch of the ghats was covered with oil lamps and candles.

As the grand *aarti* began, the crew rushed to the pandals to shoot the enchanting sight. I sat by the riverside to watch the fanfare of the much-hyped Ganga aarti. To my surprise, I found three children, each disguised as Lord Shiva, approaching me. One of them stretched out his blue palm, asking me for a coin or two. I pointed to the crew, explaining that they were shooting amidst the crowd, and told the kids that I wasn't carrying my wallet. However, not to disappoint them, I showed them a trick using an oil lamp. The sight of a television crew, cameras and shooting equipment excited the kids no end. Then they regaled us with the lore of 'Boom Boom Baba', who sat by the bank, wore black clothes, spoke English and apparently ate human flesh! The kids claimed that he was the original magician of Varanasi, and that they'd believe in my skill only if I tricked him.

The very mention of this personality shaped an image in my head. I was more interested in meeting him than in performing my magic. Immediately I shouted to the crew and called them back. They could hardly hear me amidst the reverberating sound of the conch shells. But thankfully, we did regroup soon. Briskly, we followed the kids towards that part of the ghats where Boom Boom Baba was seated. The three little Shivas elbowed the horde and paved the way for us as if they were leading an entourage.

As we walked further, we saw that the crowd had dissipated and we found ourselves in a rather eerie corner of the ghat. On one side were the ruins of an old temple that faced the river. A setting spooky yet interesting enough to make us stay. Excitedly, the children went inside the ruins and brought Boom Boom Baba out in the open.

What a sight he was! His hair was long, tangled and matted. He was draped in smelly rags and carried a small glass in his hand. When asked anything, he would only chant, '*Har Har Mahadev!*', interspersed with some phrases in broken English. It was an incredible situation, both creepy and amusing. While the crew stood stunned by his appearance, the kids began to laugh at the whole scene.

Getting to the challenge that the Shivas had posed, I snapped out of my state of wonder and quickly started looking for something to do magic with. Of course, I found my trusted rubber bands.

Leaping Rupee

A banknote jumps from one band of a stretched rubber band to another

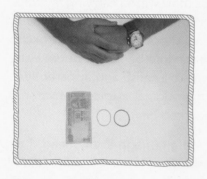

> **MATERIAL REQUIRED:**
> Two rubber bands of different colours and one banknote of any denomination.

PREPARATION:

1. Fold the note in half, lengthwise, and then again, breadthwise.
2. Now give a slim fold horizontally near the already-existing fold. Your gimmick is ready!

THE TRICK DECODED

① Ask the spectator to extend the index fingers of both their hands. Loop the rubber band around their fingers and stretch it between them.

② Hang the note at the horizontal fold on the lower length of the rubber band. And as you do so, hook the slim fold on to the upper length of the band. Do both these moves simultaneously and in a swift motion, so that the spectator fails to notice that the note is only hanging on the lower length. The spectator will think that it is hanging from the upper length of the band.

③ Pull the note down to the lower length of the band by giving it a slight jerk. The slim fold gets unhooked from the upper length as you pull the note, and it falls on the lower length of the band.

④ Unfold the note and give it to the spectator for examination.

 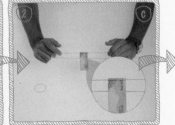

Neel's Tip: *You may avoid the last step if you do not want to let the audience notice the extra fold in the centre of the note. But given the multiple creases on a used banknote, this should not stand out.*

After this trick, Boom Boom Baba—an Aghori sadhu—proposed that I perform with a bulb. And I did! Watch the trick on our YouTube channel.

We were back in Rajasthan, in the magical city of Bundi. The magnificent Taragarh Fort that flanked the valley and stood perched like a falcon overlooking the town, greeted us as soon as we arrived.

Since we had already shot in a lot of forts in Rajasthan, we were accustomed to a certain experience. Most of the forts had struck a balance between their antique grandeur and modern luxury. They were well preserved and easily accessible, overflowing with guests, had an army of people taking care of the upkeep, with smooth driveways and tastefully curated interiors. Some also boasted of musicians who brought alive the soul of Rajasthan with their rustic notes.

But our impression began changing as soon as we set out to drive up to the Taragarh Fort. While in the city, somebody had suggested to us a meandering route that went around the hill. On this path, we found no milestones, no signboards. It was looking like the beginning of an unusual experience! The quality of the road declined—from being tar-coated to potholed to cobbled to finally ceasing to exist. A carpet of sharp stones lined a pathway that led to the fort. Surrounding it was a forbidding jungle of leafless trees that gleamed like silver in the sunlight. We all agreed, including the driver, to not return to this fort in the course of our shoot in Bundi—but little did we know that it was far from what was going to happen. The car bumped along painfully.

We finally reached the top after a heart-pounding ride. The hilltop lay deserted, not a person in sight. A narrow lane led to the main gate of the fort and we started to drive towards it, when somebody at the gate—which appeared to be shut—called out to us. He was running towards us, vigorously waving his arms and gesturing to us to go back. We pulled over and got out of the car, too puzzled to even move an inch. It turned out that as it was past 5 p.m., the fort was closed for visitors. Taragarh Fort was definitely not smacking of the kind of luxury that would invite the usual tourist. In fact, apart from our crew, just three other people were being turned away from the gate. But I wondered, how could a fort this picturesque, not have more people visiting it? Perhaps that was the key feature that drew us to the fort.

Taragarh Fort, an imposing manifestation of the grandeur of the Chauhans of Rajasthan, now lies uncared for—with dilapidated gates, vanishing pathways and a palpable strangeness in the air. During our visit, the place gave us gooseflesh. We hadn't yet encountered a place so suffused with mystery and appeal. This fort was not even part of the planned episode, but its peculiar charm seemed perfect for our show, which scouts out these unique locations. Magic had brought us there, and I felt that I needed to repay it in magical currency too, on the very same night.

So I asked the other men to join us and, with all that I could find—a stray pencil and a banknote—I performed an illusion for them. Although they couldn't enter the fort at the time, just like us, they were thrilled by the little show. They weren't expecting magic on top of a deserted hill, just as we were not expecting the intrigue of the fort. Taragarh Fort didn't disappoint any of us.

As we turned to leave, I took one last look at the gate, in search of the man who'd stood outside and implored us to retreat. But the gate was still closed, and there was no man in sight. I scanned the surroundings but found no path, other than the one we were standing on, leading to or from the gate.

Inspired by the aura of the fort, after the trick with a pencil and a note, I performed another one for our fellow visitors, who were as intrigued by the ambience as us. Watch my illusion on our YouTube channel!

Slice the Pencil

Breaking a pencil in two using a banknote

> **MATERIAL REQUIRED:**
> One pencil and a banknote of any denomination.

PREPARATION: **Place the spectator directly in front of you.**

THE TRICK DECODED

① Give a full-length, sharpened pencil to a member of the audience and ask them to hold it horizontally—one hand at either end—at about waist height, in front of them. Instruct them to hold the pencil tightly.

② Borrow a banknote from another member of the audience and fold it in half, lengthwise. Make a show of running your finger down the fold and saying how sharp it is!

③ Then, with the fold towards the floor, hold the banknote at one end between your thumb and index finger.

④ Raise the banknote above the pencil and then quickly bring it down on the pencil in a sweeping, chopping action. Just before the banknote hits the pencil, and concealed behind the banknote, swiftly extend your index finger with which you were gripping the note.

⑤ Your finger and banknote should hit the pencil at the same time and break it in half. As your hand continues its downward motion after 'slicing' the pencil, quickly retract your index finger. The pencil has been broken into two!

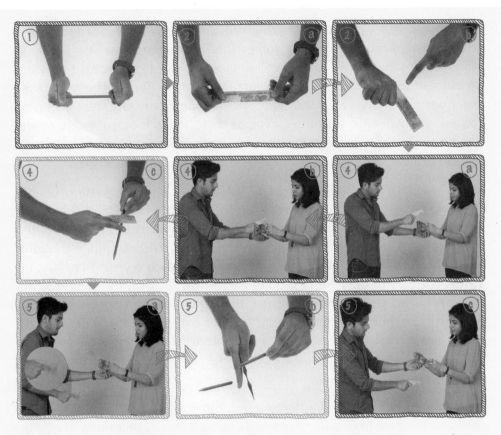

Neel's Tip: *If you do it at the right speed, no one will see you moving your finger!*

Our breathtaking experiences across north India were complemented by our stay in south India, particularly in God's Own Country, Kerala. After Kochi and Kumarakom, the crew and I made our way to Mararikulam, in the south of Kerala. Located on the shore of the Indian Ocean, this is a quaint little fishing village. We entered Mararikulam, the unmistakable smell of the sea and its fish greeting us, and drove past coconut trees filtering the sunlight, men dressed in white mundus selling their wares from kiosks, women carrying baskets filled with fish and fruit, little children scampering around. I'm not usually lethargic, but the languid pace of the beachside town grew on me in no time.

Our local guide instructed us to wake up early for the morning shoot the next day and up we were, well before sunrise, hardly having rested. Once we arrived at the beach, I was stunned to hear the cacophony and commotion at 3 a.m.—the fishermen of the village were headed to sea at this hour to return with nets full of fish by the time morning set in. In Mararikulam, the fishermen are called 'sons of the sea' because they are considered to be invincible at sea, just like pirates. Every fisherman takes one boat out and stays in the water till the sun has risen. Their skin gets etched with wrinkles, and the palms of their hands look pale due to the salt in seawater. But like pirates, they sail back merrily, singing to celebrate a good catch.

In the midst of the flurry of activity, while the crew was setting up the shooting equipment, my eyes were caught by a little boy. Hardly eleven or twelve, dressed in local attire and unaffected by the pandemonium of the fishermen, he was collecting shells on the beach. Without much thought, I walked up to him, mildly curious to know why such a young lad was up at this ungodly hour. When I inquired if he was looking for someone, he shook his head and showed me the little bag that hung from his shoulder. Inside it were, not a few, but hundreds and hundreds of shells. Since I had to rejoin the team for our shoot, I didn't interrogate him further, assuming that the shells were for some sort of game. Little did I know the secrets they held.

From the corner of my eye, I saw him continuing his pursuit, collecting shells for the next hour while the waves of the sea leapt higher and higher. At the end of the hour, the young boy stopped to stare at the water for some time before walking back. Unable to decipher this, I went up to him again.

'I can hear the sea and the fish in these shells!' he said in fluent English. And giving me a few from his collection, he ran inside a small opening among the coconut trees.

I lost sight of him and went back to the shoot. But I was fascinated by his answer and tried listening, putting a shell to my ear. Obviously, I heard nothing.

By this time, it was around 4.30 a.m. All the fishermen had gone out to sea and the beach was silent again. We waited for their return and rested on a bench till the first rays of the sun shone bright. As the boats were sighted in the sea at a distance, the locals lined up on the beach to buy the first catch of the day. We saw the sons of the sea return to shore against the gleaming yellow of the sun. Amidst the men and the fish, my eyes caught sight of the young boy again. He stood with his father, a fisherman, who was separating the fish from the net.

We continued to shoot on the beach for the next two hours and as we were wrapping up to leave, the lad came running up to me, excitement twinkling in his eyes.

I handed the shells back, the ones which he had given to me. 'I couldn't hear the sea,' I said, smiling.

He responded with a grin. 'I hear the waves when my father goes out to sea. It tells me if he has got a good catch!' With a wink, he added, 'I know why you couldn't hear the waves—you are a city boy!'

As the bustle of the fish market on the beach crescendoed, no one gathered there expected their everyday chore to get a lot more interesting. The city boy had a trick in mind!

10 to 20

A twenty-rupee note changes into a ten-rupee note, and back into a twenty-rupee note

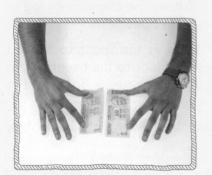

MATERIAL REQUIRED:
Two ten-rupee notes, one twenty-rupee note and a glue stick.

PREPARATION:

① Fold a ten-rupee note thrice. The ideal way to fold is to keep the picture of Mahatma Gandhi facing you, then fold the note right to left. Then right to left again, and then from the bottom to the top. The corner with the denomination should face you.

② Stick this folded square on the reverse plane of the twenty-rupee note, on the bottom-left corner.

This is your rigged note—be careful to not hand it to the spectator during the course of the trick.

THE TRICK DECODED

① Give the other ten-rupee note to the spectator for inspection. Keep the rigged twenty-rupee note with you.

② Now fold the twenty-rupee note, with the folded ten-rupee note stuck to it and hidden from the spectator. Ask the spectator to copy you and fold their ten-rupee note exactly the same way. You must fold the twenty-rupee note in such a way that you have the twenty showing on one side and the ten showing on the reverse side.

③ Take both the folded notes and put them in the spectator's hand. Make sure to not reveal the ten-rupee note stuck to the twenty-rupee note. When giving them the notes, put the ten-rupee note on their palm first and then the twenty-rupee note on top of it.

④ Ask them to close their fist. Then flip their hand so that the back of the hand faces upwards.

⑤ Then reach into their fist and pull out one of the notes, asking, 'Was this the one?' You know that the rigged note is now the one at the bottom and when you take it out of their fist, the ten-rupee side will show, facing upwards, while the banknote is actually a twenty-rupee note. If this is what happens, then you let them believe that you got it wrong.

6. Now ask them to focus on the ten-rupee note that you pulled out from their hand. Show them the ten-rupee side by holding the folded note by the edges with your middle finger and thumb so that your index finger is free to flip the note over to show that it has magically changed into a twenty-rupee note. Ask them to hold your hand as you shake the note to create a magical effect. Do not hand over this note to the spectator.

7. Ask them to open their hand—the other ten-rupee note will still be there!

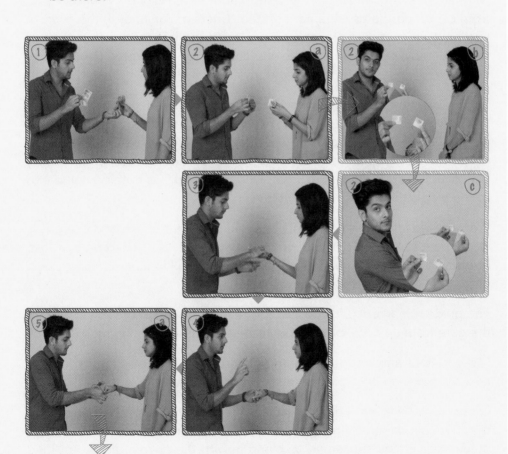

One of our most significant shoots, which summed up all that *You Got Magic* is about—not only bringing magic to the people of India, but finding the magic in them—was in Lucknow. It was the month of Ramadan and we were all set to get a taste of the celebrations in the City of Nawabs. Apart from capturing the usual fanfare on the streets of Aminabad, the heart of Lucknow, we had also planned on exploring the beautiful architecture of the city. And the Bara Imambara, one of the most celebrated structures of Lucknow, divulged to us its age-old mystery.

On an evening shoot, we were accompanied by a guide to lead us through its labyrinthine complex; we had researched about the formidable monument as well. All we knew was that the Bara Imambara had an inbuilt maze, the construction of the windows and corridors creating an illusory play of light and shadow. But what we'd imagined was nothing compared to the magic that this structure held.

We were led into a maze of dimly lit corridors by our guide, and eventually we made it to the top of the building. The dark alleys opened on to a vast, brightly lit terrace, its boundary lined with arches. I looked ahead to see a glittering Lucknow sprawled at my feet.

The guide remarked, 'Sir, you can spot every activity on the street around the gate from up here, but nobody can see you from down there.'

I was thrilled and intrigued to know more. This was exactly my kind of enchantment—an interplay of revealing and concealing.

On our way back, I led the trail, our guide bringing up the rear. He was a talkative man with an engaging sense of humour. As we walked on, the guide's voice almost seemed to blend in with the surroundings, not loud but reverberating through the walls. Although he was many paces behind us, his voice travelled with us. Just then, I turned around to find that the guide was not following us any longer. Someone from the team had seen him slip into another corridor but his words remained with us.

'Aagey jao! Aagey jao-aao-aao . . .'

Frantically, we searched for him till we found him almost 300 metres away from us—and we could still hear him whisper. The sound almost travelled to us *through* the walls. He gestured to us to wait where we were and showed us a matchbook, saying, 'Wait and watch, you'll be able to listen to me light a matchstick.'

We exchanged glances and chuckled softly. No way was he being serious, we assumed—but he was. He lit a match against the matchbook and we could clearly hear every bit of it—from strike to sizzle to spark! Then we found out that the walls of the maze in the Bara Imambara were hollow and hence, they carried sound—and a vein of magic too.

Of course the fascinating Bara Imambara and our interesting guide sparked the magic in me! Visit our YouTube channel to watch the trick that the two inspired.

Burn, Baby, Burn!

A burnt match disappears only to reappear inside the matchbook

MATERIAL REQUIRED:
A matchbook, a lighter and some Sellotape.

PREPARATION:

1. Angle any match upright from the booklet's front row. The match should stand perpendicular to the others and separate from them. Remember, do not pull it out; just bend it to a perpendicular position.

2. Light this match using the lighter, burn it for a second and blow it out.

   Later, when you hold the matchbook out to the spectator to show the unburnt matches, ensure that you pull it to the other side and cover it with your right thumb. This burnt match will be hidden from the spectator's view.

3. Stick a tiny loop of Sellotape on your left thumbnail. Ensure that it is small enough to not catch the spectator's attention. This is where you will accommodate the match that you actually light in front of the spectator.

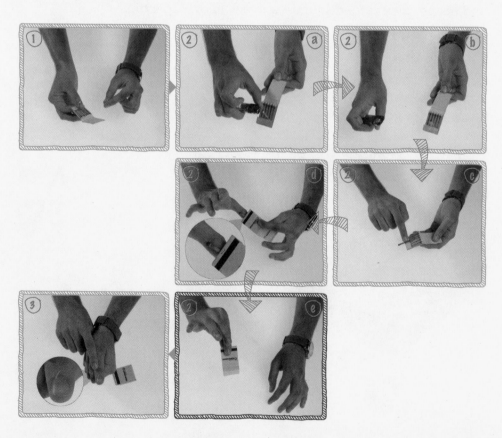

THE TRICK DECODED

1. Start the trick by showing the matchbook to the spectator. Hold the matchbook in your right hand, pinning the burnt match so that your right thumb conceals it.

2. Now ask the spectator to pull out a match and light it against the booklet's striking pad.

3. Close the matchbook, releasing the hidden match that you had held with your right thumb, back into the book. While closing the matchbook, ensure that the back of the book is angled towards the spectator. This will conceal the view of the burnt match going back into the book.

4. Keep the closed matchbook in the spectator's hand and ask them to immediately cover it with the other hand.

5. With your right hand, take the match that the spectator just lit. Extinguish the lit match by shaking it back and forth. As long as you see the smoke, continue to shake your right hand as you secretly prepare to slip it to your left thumbnail, where you have already stuck tape to accommodate it. As you do so, it will look like the lit match has vanished.

6. Then ask the spectator to open the matchbook and let them be surprised at the sight of the burnt match inside. When they try to remove it, they'll be stunned further—the match has reattached itself.

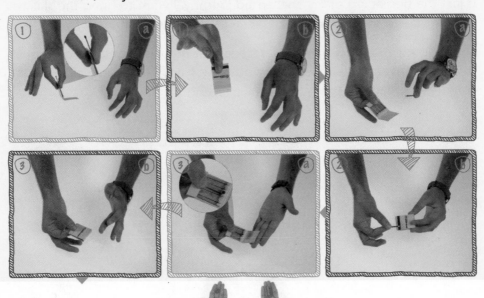

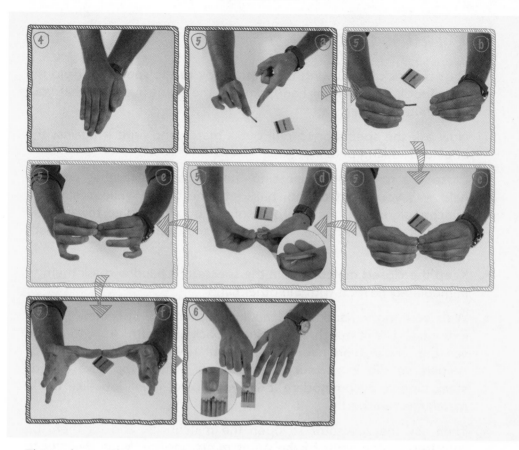

Things have taken a quick turn for me, thanks to *You Got Magic*—but this is just the beginning of my enchanted journey. I want to bring the skill set for magic, and the happiness that it can spread, to each one of you.

Shooting for the show made me realize that if you set out on your quest, India will never disappoint you. And now I am wandering all over the country, my magic in tow.

Conclusion
PERFORM YOUR OWN SHOW

Here I describe two easy tricks that you can perform anywhere and for anyone. They're simple and don't require an elaborate set-up or too many gimmicks, but they'll leave a lasting impression. Remember—a magician is set apart from the rest by how he exhibits his magic. It isn't the magnificence of one's tricks or the size of the props or the duration of the performance that makes a trick effective. It is, instead, the way a magician interacts with his audiences, hypnotizing them for a while and transporting them to the world of the surreal, where the real is galaxies away from the imagined. That is the true purpose and strength of magic—and anyone can have it. Even you!

Connected

K♣
K♣

The magician astounds the spectator by guessing the correct four-digit number that the spectator arrives at after some calculations, without knowing the original number

CASTING THE ILLUSION:

Go up to anyone and tell them that you visited them in their dreams. And to prove it, ask them to open the calculator application on their phone. Ask them to punch in random numbers and, after some math, they land on a sum. Ask them to check the total and then lock their phone. Then say to them, 'In the dream, I met you and you said that you would take out the calculator and type in random digits. And that you will land up on a four-digit number—which is 1089!'

And that will blow their mind because that will be the exact number that they would have landed on!

THE TRICK DECODED

What is the math that you have to ask the spectator to carry out to always arrive at the sum 1089?

'Punch in any three-digit number. Subtract it with the inverse of that number—but do it in such a way that the result will be a whole number and not a negative value. So if your number is 789 and the inverse is 987, then you should rearrange the equation so that it becomes 987−789. Then whatever the difference is, add it to its inverse.'

The sum will always come to 1089!

Mirror Me

A bar bet that will impress anyone

Play a game with your spectator-participant, in which they have to mirror you for thirty seconds. If they can complete the bet, then you buy them a drink. And if they can't, then you still buy them a drink. Well, you see, they *won't* win!

THE TRICK DECODED

1. Keep a glass with some liquid in it near you and make sure that your spectator has one as well.

2. Make some random movements for about ten seconds and then take a sip from your glass.

3. Put the glass down and say something silly. Then, make some more random hand gestures and proceed to take another sip.

4. But this time, don't swallow the liquid. Act like you gulped it down and put the glass aside.

5. After another random gesture with your hand, take your glass and pour the liquid that was in your mouth back into it. Your participant won't be able to do that!

Neel's Tip: *So now that you've won the bet and broken the ice, the rest is up to you.*

Acknowledgements

My journey in the realm of creativity, magic and illusion has just started. And it seems from the encouragement I keep receiving that I am on the right path. No one knows what will happen in the years to come, but what we do in the present definitely has an impact on our future. The past has shaped my present and there are several people and incidents that have had lasting influences on my life, leaving indelible imprints. These imprints make up my armoury of blueprints that help me in different situations today, and will no doubt continue to do so in the future.

My parents, without whose support I would not have been able to pursue my passion, and this book would not have been written.

All my friends at the Doon School—especially my housemates, and the fellow members of the football and gymnastics teams.

My housemaster at the Doon School, Gurusharan Singh—a man of exceptional talent, amazing creativity and great common sense—under whose guidance I excelled at sports and music.

B.C. Chamola, the succeeding housemaster, who cheered me on to demonstrate my skills to him and his family, and whose children became great friends with me.

A meeting with the world-renowned illusionist Jason Randal, which strengthened my passion for magic into resolve.

An encounter with the Big Daddy of magic, James Randi, who further motivated me on my way.

Wade Davis of Viacom Inc., who helped me make up my mind about a career in the field of media. A skiing and sports enthusiast, Mr Davis helped me understand that learning takes place as much in the outdoors as in the classroom.

Ashok Advani of the Business India Group, who left a deep impression on me. Incredibly approachable, he provided some invaluable advice to my younger self.

Sunjoy Waddhwa and Comall Waddhwa of Sphere Origins who have constantly fortified my actions.

Prannoy Roy, an encounter with whom changed my life. He greeted me with unexpected enthusiasm, and was willing to hear me out.

Smeeta Chakrabarti, CEO of NDTV Good Times, who, along with her team—including Annu Singh and many others—joined me in debating how we could bring magic to Indian television. Thus, intertwining food, travel and illusion, the unique brainchild behind *You Got Magic* was conceived.

Amish Tripathi for being so encouraging, always.

The very many people who have helped me during the course of my corporate events and productions for giants in the field, like Oracle India, Britannia Industries, Canon India, Lipton, Shree Cement, etc. I would like to thank them all, for each event has been special to me, where I've had the chance to innovate and reach out to the audience with illusions that could wow them.

The various educational institutions across the country to which I have been invited, to speak to the students about innovation and out-of-the-box thinking. These interactions have been fulfilling and invigorating. Additionally, the TEDx Talks, in Mumbai and Bangalore, have given me the perfect platform to present my views on magic and illusion in the new-age India.

Our team at Media Network Pvt. Ltd, who has made the show a reality. I am especially thankful to Mrigashree Pant and Akriti Suman, who have helped me throughout the planning stage of the book in putting together the tricks and photographs that have been presented here. My gratitude is due to Aishwarya Kandpal for her contribution, and to Praveen Kumar for the logistical management. Their creative inputs at every step have been of the utmost importance, as has been Neerja Kohli's presence, who painstakingly took down notes.

Sohini Mitra from Penguin Random House India for commissioning the book, Kankana Basu for meticulously editing it, Neelima P Aryan for the splendid design and Piya Kapur for being the marketing genius that she is.

And last but not least, my entire family. My grandmother, my uncle; my brother, Suryavir, and Srishti; my nana and nani; my aunts and all my cousins—who have been the initial guinea pigs for my various experiments in magic and illusion.

My thanks are due to all.